HOW TO TALK TO ANYONE WITH EASE

21 ACTIONABLE SKILLS FOR YOUNG ADULTS TO TACKLE SOCIAL ANXIETY AND MAKE FRIENDS IN THE AI-DRIVEN DIGITAL AGE

RENÉ CLAYTON

INKBYTE PUBLISHING LLC

Library of Congress Control Number:
ISBN: 978-1-966339-00-7 (pbbk)
ISBN: 978-1-966339-01-4 (hbbk)
Printed in the United States

To every reader who discovers a part of their story
within these pages

CONTENTS

PART FIVE
AI & US: NO BS GUIDE

PREFACE

PIVOT POINT

Why this book and why now?

How did it feel when the world shut down in March 2020, and suddenly, every connection, each friendship—had to be rebuilt through a screen? There is no question that early in 2020, the world we knew had changed forever. It completely shut down from Hong Kong to Sydney to Alaska to Chicago, Morocco, Reykjavik, and Cape Town—one hundred percent of us were affected by the shutdown when the pandemic hit. The significance of that time has shaped how we interact with other people more than at any other time in human history.

I remember my company telling us we would be back at work in two weeks, and at the time, we thought that sounded fantastic! We would have no commute, work in our pajamas for a few weeks, and then return to normal. That was not the outcome. Life and how we connect with each other changed in ways we never could have imagined.

Communicating on a smartphone or laptop screen became the only way we communicated with people for months. Handshakes turned into faraway waves, sometimes fist bumps, and at one time, massive amounts of people were wearing masks, and here it began. Even the best communicators lost a bit of themselves. We were alone (or with our immediate family), just graduating high school, or perhaps entering college "virtually" as a freshman or starting that new job "remotely." Many people "lost" their ability to connect with others like we always had before—eye to eye, in person—and learned to hide behind a screen. Social restrictions during the pandemic hampered many young adults' social development, impacting their comfort with in-person interactions and making friends.

My journey and thoughts around this topic began on March 13, 2020, when I went from working daily at a large corporate office, traveling around the country every month -- to staying at home 90% of the time. I became comfortable with isolation, and even now, I tend to choose to stay home over jumping back into a packed social life. It was during this time that, while often hidden, my social anxiety kicked into high gear.

For those of you who were going through big life moments and tried to adjust during and post-pandemic—graduating high school, starting college, landing a new job, or even getting engaged—things played out in ways you did not expect. These milestones unfolded (or didn't) in ways none of us could have predicted. Along the way, many of us lost touch with how to handle social dynamics. Think back to how you felt. Conversations perhaps became complicated, and the art of small talk and talking to new people is less straightforward. Almost forgotten.

On top of all this, we are in the midst of a massive shift in the tech world. With artificial intelligence (AI), Web3, generative AI, and robotics advancing at breakneck speed, we are living through a revolution unlike anything before. These technologies are not just tools; they're reshaping how we connect, communicate, and see the world around us. What's taking place now with technological advancements is monumental and much more than new gadgets; it's redefining how we interact, and that change is happening faster than we can blink.

In this book, "How to Talk to Anyone with Ease," I'm driven to empower young adults from all backgrounds to excel in communication, especially in navigating conversations in today's digital world. After the last few years, it became apparent that we might need to 're-learn' how to steer social dynamics in Our present-day reality. Whether it's connecting face-to-face or through a screen, making new friends, managing social anxiety (even if it's new to you), or building lasting relationships—these are abilities we rely on now more than ever. That's exactly why this book was created: to help you find your way through it all and come out on the other side as the best version of yourself.

INTRODUCTION

Here's the truth: You don't have to force yourself to talk to others, battle your anxiety, or painstakingly build relationships out of obligation—you genuinely want to. This desire is woven into the very fabric of who you are, an intrinsic spark capable of transforming your connections all on its own. Some of the most intriguing people I know aren't the smartest, the most attractive, wildly popular, or the life of the party. What sets them apart is one simple truth: they have a desire to engage with others. And deep down, so do you. Say goodbye to the stress of striking up conversations—this book equips you with everything you need to connect with anyone confidently.

The key to developing strong relationships with people is tapping into your natural desire to connect. When you acknowledge and act on your urge to reach out, you become available for conversations and experiences that can unexpectedly enrich your life. It's not about forcing interactions or putting on a facade; it's about being authentic and letting your true self connect with others. So go ahead, send that message, start that chat, and watch how your world expands.

Navigating today's communication environment presents unique challenges. While technology has facilitated unprecedented levels of connectivity, it has surprisingly made new friendships more elusive.

Social anxiety, awkwardness, and the struggle to form significant relationships are common issues. These difficulties have only intensified in a world where digital communication and artificial intelligence (AI) dominate. Young adults often feel disconnected, even when they are constantly connected.

The advancement of technology has changed the way we interact. Social media, smartphones, and AI have made communication more accessible but also impersonal. We spend more time behind screens and less time engaging in face-to-face conversations. A seven-country study in 2020 notes, "Recent accounts suggest that levels of social anxiety may be rising. Studies have indicated that greater social media usage, increased digital connectivity and visibility, and more options for non-face-to-face communication are associated with higher levels of social anxiety". It shows that while technology connects us, it also isolates us.

I aim to offer 21 actionable skills (and more) to cut through the noise and empower readers to communicate confidently, build meaningful relationships, and tackle social anxiety. The book is tailored specifically for young adults, considering the unique pressures and opportunities in today's constantly connected, digitally driven, and AI-powered era.

Effective communication is critical to happiness. Studies have shown that people with strong emotional ties are happier. Improving your social skills can enhance your relationships and overall well-being.

What if 21 insights could change the way you approach your future?

This book covers a spectrum of essential tools designed to enhance your communication. It reveals the must-have skills young adults must embody to crush it and assemble an epic circle of awesome friends. Let's make conversations exciting and less anxious!

Listed are 21 tips *(within the book, and not in order)* discussed in the book to help you speak confidently, make friends, connect authentically, and more.

1. Use Open Body Language and Cues
2. Social Perceptiveness
3. Show Interest with a Question
4. Listen More, Speak Less
5. Start with Shared Experiences
6. Mirror Their Energy
7. Stay Curious
8. Make Eye Contact (But Don't Stare!)
9. Give True Compliments
10. Share a Little About Yourself
11. Find Common Interests
12. Focus on Positivity
13. Expand your Charisma
14. Stay Present and Avoid Overthinking
15. Celebrate Progress, Not Perfection
16. Elevate Emotional Intelligence
17. Transform Social Awareness
18. Keeping Learning
19. Hobbies and Volunteering
20. Understand how digital and AI are in the mix
21. (the MOST important one) Be Yourself, Not Who You Think They Want

This is my invitation to revolutionize your communicative abilities in this digital era and beyond. With fresh perspectives, practical advice, and innovative strategies, I aim to walk you through a guidance of excellence in all your conversational endeavors, regardless of your level of social confidence.

As we embark on this trek together, I am reminded of my own experiences and the challenges I have overcome. I sincerely hope that by sharing this knowledge, I can assist you in breaking down the barriers to effective communication, reflecting my lifelong dedication to helping others.

Are you ready to transform your relationship with the world around you? We can explore the steps to becoming more confident and connected. The path to better communication and amazing relationships starts now.

PART ONE
SIGNALS AND STARTERS

CHAPTER ONE

THE SILENT CONVERSATION: YOUR BODY SPEAKS LOUDER THAN WORDS

E very time we swipe, scroll, or step into a room, our bodies speak for us—sometimes louder than our words ever could.

Meeting someone new can be like dropping a single pebble into a still pond. That first little splash—the quick smile, the easy "hello," or a shared laugh—creates waves that spread, often further than you'd expect. One small moment can kick off a whole chain of events, connecting you to people, opportunities, and ideas you'd never imagined.

It's like this: each interaction is part of a bigger story, where every affiliation you make has the power to ripple out. A quick chat with someone at a party leads to a new friend who introduces you to a job lead or a casual acquaintance who knows someone working on a project you would love. Sociologist Mark Granovetter talks about this idea as "the strength of weak ties"—even those loose connections can open up whole new worlds.

And that's the magic. Every small interaction has the potential to grow into something much more significant. By just showing up and putting a little effort into each encounter, you're setting off ripples that can shape your personal and professional life in ways you can't always see immediately but will feel down the line.

Let's begin with the basics. Before you even walk into an event, set a goal. Stand up tall, take a breath, no matter how you feel, and relax. Are you attending a party, a networking event, or a family reunion? Think about your intention ahead of time. Do you want to make a new friend, rekindle an old friendship, land a new job, or get caught up with your long-lost cousin Jed? Clarifying what you want to achieve is the foundation of success. When your mind has a clear vision, your actions naturally align to bring that goal within reach.

With a clear vision of your desired outcome, it's time to plan your approach. Understand the relevance of why you are going where you are going or doing what you are doing. Consider details of your outfit, the weather, and whether it's a standing or seated gathering. Preparing these strategies in advance helps build confidence and puts you at ease. For example, if I'm heading to a party, I'll enter confidently, pause to scan the room for a familiar face or the refreshment table, and proceed with purpose. This small and critical preparation shifts the tone for a positive experience.

By understanding three distinct concepts—body language, cues, and social perceptiveness—we will begin to unpack how they intersect. They are related, and each plays a role in how we interact smoothly when meeting or engaging with people.

YOUR BODY TALKS

The fascinating aspect of body language is that it's like learning a secret code—but most of us haven't had someone to teach us all the tricks. Instead, we pick it up by watching others and figuring it out as we go. Sometimes, that leads to funny moments, like when people think you're upset just because you're tired, or they mistake your thoughtfulness for disinterest when you break eye contact. Imagine the possibilities when you know how to guide that message yourself!

Early in my career, as one of the few women in the technology department, I thought staying serious—avoiding smiles and keeping my guard up—was the best way to blend in. Then, one day, a mentor gently suggested that showing a bit more warmth and openness could work to my advantage. At first, I wasn't sure how to take it, but once I started leaning into that advice, I saw just how powerful a simple smile and openness could be. It changed how I connected with others and ultimately shaped my career in ways I hadn't imagined.

Body language isn't a secret code set in stone. It's simply how we express ourselves, and when you use it with purpose, it can help you come across as confident, build ties with others, and bring good energy to any conversation. For young adults, conquering body language is like having a superpower in social settings. It doesn't just affect how others see you; it influences how you feel about yourself.

In this chapter, we will discuss how your body language shapes the energy of interaction, whether face-to-face, over a video call, or even through text. We'll also dive into some easy-to-apply tips to help you become more aware of your body's silent messages and how to adjust them to match the vibe you want to establish. Ready to unlock the secrets of nonverbal communication? Let's go.

DROP THE MIC: THE POWER OF FIRST IMPRESSIONS

There's a saying that goes, "You never get a second chance to make a first impression." While it might sound dramatic, there's a lot of truth to it. First impressions happen fast—within the first twenty seconds of meeting someone, they've already formed an opinion about you. And guess what? Most of that impression has nothing to do with what you say and everything to do with how you carry yourself.

But here's the good news: you don't need to fear the first impression. It's not about perfection or being someone you're not; it's about being aware of the signals you're sending and learning how to align them with who you are. Making a solid first impression is a skill; like any skill, it can be learned, practiced, and refined. With just a little guidance, you'll discover how to approach every introduction confidently and easily, knowing you have the tools to create meaningful connections. Relax—you've got this.

Let's look at a real-life example. Imagine a student named Mia walking into a new classroom. She's nervous, but she doesn't want anyone to know that. Without thinking, she walks in with her head down, arms crossed over her chest and makes a beeline for the back of the room. To her, she's just trying to get through the day. But to everyone else, it looks like she's either mad, uninterested, or doesn't want to be approached. Her body language—closed off and withdrawn—sends out energy that keeps others from engaging with her, even though she may want to make new friends.

Now, picture another student, Nathan, walking into the same room. He's also nervous, but he's learned to adjust his body language to project confidence. He walks in with his shoulders back, head held high, and a relaxed expression. He scans the room and says "hi" to a few people before he finds a seat. His body language sends an entirely different message: he's open, approach-able, and ready to engage, even though he might feel the same jitters as Mia.

The difference between Mia and Nathan isn't about who they are as people, it's all about the signals they're sending with their bodies. The beautiful thing is that body language is something you can control and tweak to match the impression you want to make.

What Makes a Great First Impression?

So, what are the key elements of body language that create a strong first impression?

Here is a breakdown:

- **Posture:** How you stand or sit says a lot about your feelings. When you slouch or hunch over, it gives the impression that you're disinterested or lack confidence. On the flip side, standing up straight with your shoulders back instantly makes you appear more confident and engaged. Even when you're sitting, having an open, upright posture can make a world of difference.
- **Facial Expressions:** Your face is one of the first things people notice about you. Are you smiling? Frowning? Do you look relaxed or tense? A neutral or slightly positive facial expression—one that doesn't scream forced excitement—goes a long way in making you appear friendly and approachable.
- **Eye Contact:** This one can be complicated, especially if you're nervous, but making eye contact is key in connecting with others. When you look someone in the eye, it shows that you're present and engaged. Conversely, avoiding it can make you seem distant or uninterested.

- **Cues:** What you do with your hands also matters. Fidgeting, crossing your arms, or constantly checking your phone can make you seem anxious or disengaged. Using open gestures and keeping your hands visible and relaxed helps convey warmth and confidence.
- **Energy and Movement:** Your overall energy can be sensed by the way you move. Walking into a room with deliberate, steady movements shows that you're in control. Rushing in or shuffling around nervously might give off an anxious vibe.

How First Impressions Set the Tone for Every Conversation

The way you enter a conversation sets the tone for the rest of the exchange. If your body language is receptive, it invites others to approach you with the same energy. This creates a feedback loop. When you exude warmth, people are more likely to return those feelings, making the conversation flow more naturally.

Unfortunately, we are not always aware of the body language we're giving off. Maybe you're at a party, and you're feeling a bit nervous. Your instinct might be to stand against the wall and look into your phone. To you, it feels like a protective move, but to others, it can signal that you're closed off or not interested in talking. Understanding how your body language is perceived can help you avoid sending the wrong message.

When you want to establish a friendly and optimistic tone in a conversation, think about how you feel and are presenting yourself. Even if you're feeling unsure, simply standing tall, and smiling can change how others respond to you—and increase your confidence in the process. It's all about radiating a strong impression that puts people at ease while leaving them feeling encouraged.

DECODING FACIAL EXPRESSIONS AND CUES

Facial expressions are perhaps the most direct way we communicate our feelings and intentions, often conveying emotions more accurately than words. They act as universal signals that can be understood across different cultures and contexts, making them a powerful tool for anyone looking to improve their social skills. For instance, a smile is universally recognized as a sign of friendliness, while a frown indicates displeasure or sadness. These expressions are often involuntary, reflecting our true emotions even when we try to hide them. Gestures are a type of non-verbal cue, and cues can encompass a wider range of signals beyond just physical movements.

Micro-expressions, those fleeting facial movements that occur in less than a second, can reveal a person's true feelings. They are so brief that they often go unnoticed, yet they provide a window into someone's sincere emotions. For example, a quick flash of anger might appear in someone's eyes or a brief tightening of the jaw. Learning to recognize these subtle cues can help you understand what someone is feeling, even if they're saying otherwise. According to research, micro-expressions are universal and consistent across different cultures, making them a reliable indicator of emotion. They are central non-verbal communication tools that convey emotional states and significantly impact others' emotions, cognition, and behavior.

A tightened jaw can identify anger, flared nostrils, and narrowed eyes. These signals show that someone is upset or frustrated. Surprise is characterized by raised eyebrows, widened eyes, and an open mouth, indicating that something unexpected has happened.

Here are essential warm cues:

- A big smile that reaches your eyes
- Raising your eyebrows at an interesting moment

- Gentle eye contact with occasional breaks
- Natural triple nod when listening
- Open palms and visible hands
- Simple affirming words ("I see," "mm-hmm")
- Relaxed shoulders and slight forward lean

Recognizing and understanding facial expressions can substantially enhance your social interactions. It lets you respond empathetically, create robust links with people, and manage social dynamics. Being attuned to these non-verbal cues can make all the difference regardless of the setting.

ENHANCING NONVERBAL COMMUNICATION SKILLS

Have you ever been in a conversation where you felt an instant bond with someone as if you both were effortlessly on the same wavelength? You might have wondered what created that sense of mutual understanding and ease. Much of this magic lies in nonverbal communication, particularly with your eyes.

Picture yourself meeting someone for the first time in a busy pickleball store. Your eyes meet as you engage in conversation, and you feel an unspoken tie forming. This is the power of eye contact—a silent yet potent tool in your communication arsenal.

Eye contact is one of the most powerful nonverbal cues in communication. When you look someone in the eye, you're not just seeing them; you're engaging more authentically. Making eye contact lays the foundation for trust. It shows them you're fully engaged and care about what they're saying. In contrast, avoiding eye contact can make you appear disinterested.

Demonstrating attentiveness shows that you are fully present in the conversation. This attentiveness is critical in professional settings, where being attentive and present boosts your credibility. Eye contact also conveys confidence and sincerity. Meeting someone's gaze without hesitation suggests that you are somewhat self-assured.

Additionally, eye contact enhances emotional attachment. If you look into someone's eyes, you can often sense their emotions, whether it's joy, sadness, or excitement. These feelings can enhance the link between you and the other person, making the interaction more meaningful. It's no wonder that eye contact is often described as the window to the soul.

The impact of eye contact varies across different settings. In job interviews, sustaining eye contact demonstrates confidence and engagement, significantly influencing the interviewer's perception of you. It shows that you are confident and in control. In romantic settings, it communicates interest and affection, creating an intensified relationship with your partner. In group discussions, distributing eye contact among participants ensures that everyone feels included and valued.

Practicing eye contact can improve your ability to use this powerful tool effectively. One simple exercise is to practice in front of a mirror. Look into your own eyes and hold the gaze for a few seconds, then look away and return your gaze.

KEY ELEMENTS OF SOCIAL PERCEPTIVENESS

Social perceptiveness is the art of tuning into others, determining what's left unsaid, and grasping the underlying feelings, dynamics, and contexts. It's a skill that turns a conversation from mere words into a rich exchange of meaning. For those who master it, social perceptiveness can transform the way they interact with anyone. I would consider it to be an invisible but powerful social compass.

Decoding Unspoken Signals

At the heart of social perceptiveness lies emotional awareness. We often think of communication as a verbal exchange, yet our emotions speak a language of their own. People communicate how they're feeling through words and subtle, often involuntary expressions— a flicker in the eyes, a tiny shift in body language, the faintest tension in a smile. Socially perceptive people notice these subtleties. They understand that sometimes, the most important things are communicated in silence.

Emotional awareness isn't about playing detective or prying into others' minds. Rather, it's about adapting to the small, nuanced ways emotions manifest. Recognizing these cues doesn't just broaden our understanding of others; it also builds trust. People are likely to communicate honestly when they feel seen and understood. When someone leans in while talking, it signals interest. A raised eyebrow might indicate curiosity or skepticism. Understanding these subtle signals allows you to adjust your approach, making your responses more attuned and impactful.

Adapting Your Body Language Based on the Room

Context sensitivity is another crucial aspect of social perceptiveness. Every social interaction occurs within a distinctive context, defined by cultural norms, unspoken expectations, and each participant's roles. The way you engage with a close friend over coffee differs vastly from how you'd present yourself in a formal job interview or at a cultural event. Contexts shape our behavior and subtly shape what's considered appropriate or respectful.

Understanding context requires us to 'read the room' to take stock of social cues that reveal how others are feeling and what's expected at that moment. Imagine attending a dinner party where everyone seems reserved, perhaps out of respect for a recent loss or a challenging topic that's been brought up. A socially perceptive person would adjust their tone, choosing words with sensitivity and perhaps refraining from lighthearted jokes that may seem out of place. They understand that context can be as dynamic as the individuals in the room, shifting with the undercurrents of group sentiment.

Being able to interpret these signals helps you decide how to navigate the conversation. Should you start by addressing everyone equally, or should you try to engage the detached person more to bring them into the fold? Or maybe it's a sign that the group's vibe isn't as cohesive as it could be, and you can adjust your approach accordingly.

Sometimes, the room's vibe can shift during a conversation, and being able to pick up on those shifts is crucial. If you're talking to someone and notice their body language becoming more closed off— like they start crossing their arms, turning away, or avoiding eye contact—that's a clue that something has changed. Maybe the topic has made them uncomfortable, or perhaps they're simply losing interest. The key is to be flexible. When you sense a change in someone's body language, you can adjust your approach by asking a question, changing the topic, or even checking in to ensure they're okay.

For instance, during a group discussion, you might notice that someone who was previously actively participating has suddenly gone quiet, with their arms folded and their gaze averted. It could be a sign that they're feeling left out, confused, or frustrated. By acknowledging their silence—maybe with a simple "Hey, what do you think?"—you can re-engage them and bring the conversation back to a place where everyone feels included.

Just as it's important to read other people's body language, it's equally important to adjust your own based on what you observe. If you walk into a room with calm and quiet energy, walking in with too much enthusiasm—loud talking, exaggerated gestures, and rapid movements—could throw off the vibe. On the other hand, if the room is buzzing with high energy, and you come in looking stiff and reserved, you might come across as out of place or disconnected.

It's not about copying others but adjusting to make you feel in sync with the group's dynamic. When your body language fits the vibe, people are more likely to feel comfortable with you, and conversations will flow more easily.

Another key point to consider is how much physical space you take up. In some social settings, like a casual hangout with friends, you might feel more comfortable spreading out, leaning back, or taking up more physical space. But in other situations, like a formal meeting or when someone else is leading a discussion, taking up too much—whether by standing too close to others or using big, sweeping gestures—can come across as dominating or disrespectful. Being mindful of personal space and adapting your body language to fit the situation shows that you're not only confident but also considerate of others.

In a world where young adults are often quick to speak but slow to listen, those who master the art of reading body language and social cues stand out. Socially perceptive individuals can tune into unspoken emotions, instinctively knowing when to listen, engage, and step back. Their empathy and understanding bring a refreshing depth to interactions, making others feel truly seen and heard. This perceptiveness becomes second nature with practice, allowing you to navigate social arenas easily.

Time to Reflect

- How does my default body language change when I feel confident versus insecure, and how can I consciously adjust it?
- Practice mindful observation.
- Think about your facial expressions.
- Monitor your physical presence in various situations.
- Consider your facial expressions at rest.
- Think about your energy level in different contexts.

CHAPTER TWO

IGNITING CONNECTIONS THROUGH SMALL TALK

There's one topic everyone loves to talk about: themselves. It's true—people's favorite subject is often their own lives because it makes them feel heard. You've struck gold if you can create a comfortable zone where they feel free to open up.

Now, imagine this scenario: You're at a friend's rooftop dinner in the city, surrounded by laughter and animated conversations, but you feel a knot of anxiety in your stomach. The thought of starting a conversation feels as frightening as scaling a mountain. You watch others mingle, wondering why it seems so effortless for them. This can be a familiar feeling for many young adults. While small talk might seem unimportant, it is indeed a necessary skill. In this chapter, we'll walk you through how to tackle the art of small talk, starting with fun and simple icebreakers.

THE POWER OF REAL TALK

This book was designed with one goal: to help you confidently talk to anyone. The secret? Start small. Those little conversations are the building blocks of great social interactions. Sometimes, the pressure to be exciting or engaging in person can feel tremendous, especially when you've spent years communicating through screens. But real-life conversations perhaps are not as polished; they don't have to be grand or life-changing to be significant. Everyday interactions—greeting a stranger, a quick chat with a classmate, or a friendly exchange with a coworker—are valuable and essential steps toward confidence in social situations.

As stated in previous pages, practicing small conversations is like exercising a muscle. Each interaction, no matter how minor it may seem, reinforces your social skills, helping you feel more natural over time. It's tempting to brush off the value of these small, everyday exchanges, but they hold a quiet power that's often underestimated. By acknowledging and valuing them, you're slowly building up your ability to connect in a positive, low-pressure way.

BREAK THE ICE

Remember to "smile" when you meet people, whether in person or online, and it will help you ease into a conversation. Icebreakers are important in breaking initial barriers and setting a comfortable conversation tone. An effective opening can transform an awkward silence into a dynamic dialogue. It's like the key that unlocks the door. Icebreakers work because they provide a gentle nudge, making it easier to start conversations. They help people feel a sense of camaraderie and openness.

Dr. Gillian Sandstrom, a psychologist from the University of Sussex, found that even brief, friendly interactions with strangers can do wonders for our well-being. Her research shows that small social moments—like chatting with a barista—can boost your mood, increase your energy, and make you feel happier overall. It's a reminder that even the most minor connections can greatly impact how we feel.

Examples of effective icebreakers vary depending on the context. It is important to ask open-ended questions, as it helps uncover insights. A first encounter with a total stranger could be somewhat uncomfortable. Until we take the time to get to know one another, we are all strangers. Asking questions can be the only way to understand someone. For instance, you might ask, "What keeps you busy outside of your work/school?" This relevant and engaging question invites the other person to share their passions. At a party, " The food at this party is awesome! What's your favorite dish?" is a solid choice. It's straightforward and opens the door to further conversation.

The psychology behind icebreakers lies in their ability to create a safe space for interaction. They reduce the fear of rejection by offering a low-risk way to start talking. People respond positively to icebreakers because they ease the initial tension and signal friendliness.

A friendly tone of voice can make you sound warm and inviting, encouraging the other person to respond similarly. To help you feel prepared, here's a list of universal questions that can be used in almost any situation:

- Hi, how are you?
- Let me guess what you do! (leads to curiosity and laughter)
- Neat event, right? What brought you here?
- What's keeping you busy these days?
- What's your favorite way to spend a weekend?

- The most interesting movie recently was (insert movie name). Did you get a chance to see it?

Or statements are equally as powerful:

- This dessert is fantastic because...
- I love playing Pickleball, but I am a terrible player...

Try this exercise: Engage in a conversation with someone you do not know well. Make it your goal to learn three new things about them and reflect on what went well or did not. Over time, these small efforts add up, making you more attuned to you and others.

Combining these elements, thoughtful conversation starters, and context-appropriate questions creates a welcoming atmosphere for dialogue. This will assist the other person in feeling secure and open the door to discussing mutual friends or interests. During events with your current friends, "What's new with you?" paired with a warm tone and attentive listening can lead to incredible shared experiences.

Later in the book, we will discuss how online interactions, such as video calls, require a slightly different approach. When you ask, "What's been going on in your world?" ensure your tone is enthusiastic. Use emojis or exclamation points to convey warmth and interest. Similarly, in video calls, maintain eye contact with the camera, smile, and nod to show you're engaged.

Taking the above actions will help you become skilled at small talk by helping you understand the importance of these first steps and how to use the skills. Remember, the goal is to make the other person feel comfortable and valued.

FROM CHIT-CHAT TO REAL TALK

Creating memorable moments that stick with you and the person you're speaking with can be the beginning of something special. Think back to when a conversation left a lasting impression on you. Chances are, it went beyond surface-level topics. Engaging in meaningful dialogue helps you better understand others and promotes closeness.

Rapport is essential for any relationship. When you engage in richer conversations, you signal that you are willing to be authentic, encouraging the other person to do the same. This mutual exchange builds a foundation of trust and shows that you value their thoughts and feelings. Over time, these richer connections can evolve into reciprocal relationships. Moving past small talk is key, whether it's a friendship, professional colleague, or romantic relationship.

Active listening and thoughtful responses are also essential. When someone shares something with you, really listen. Avoid planning your next response while they're speaking. Instead, laser focus on their words, respond thoughtfully and listen carefully. This might mean paraphrasing what they've said to show you understand. For instance, if they mention a challenging situation, you could say, "It sounds like training your new puppy (or current topic) has been demanding. How have you been managing it?" This not only keeps the conversation going but also demonstrates empathy.

Sharing personal anecdotes or experiences is another effective way to strengthen conversations. When you share a bit about yourself, you nurture an environment for mutual vulnerability. It doesn't have to be something exceptionally personal. Even sharing a story about a recent challenge or success can make the conversation engaging. For example, if someone mentions they've been traveling, you might share a memorable travel experience of your own. It creates a sense of connection and encourages the other person to expand further.

Asking thought-provoking questions can steer conversations toward more substantial topics. Instead of sticking to generic questions, try asking about the other person's values, beliefs, or aspirations. A few of my favorite questions are, "What is a memory you never want to let go of?" or "Where is a place you always wanted to visit and why?" can encourage deeper reflection and sharing. These questions allow you to learn what truly matters to the other person and make better connections. Thought-provoking questions show that you care more than surface-level details, making the conversation more meaningful.

Finding common ground or shared interests can also help transition to diverse topics. When you discover mutual hobbies, passions, or experiences, it becomes easier to engage in significant dialogue. For instance, if you both enjoy a particular interest, you can discuss related experiences.

Here are some examples of questions that can help transition from small talk to more substantial conversations and ensure you are curious:

- From "What do you do?" to "What do you like to do on the weekend?"
- From "Where are you from?" to "What's the most unusual/unique fact of the state you are from?"
- From "Did you have a good week?" to "What's been an exciting experience this week?"

These initial curious questions invite the other person to share more about themselves, their values, and their world! Just be INTERESTED in other people.

Maintaining engagement in solid conversations requires a few strategic approaches. Reflective listening is one technique. By paraphrasing what the other person says, you show that you are paying attention and value their input. For example, if they share a story about a recent accomplishment, you might respond with, "So, you managed to complete your workout goals!" That's impressive! How did you pull it off, or what was your motivation?" This validates their experience and encourages them to elaborate. Recently, a new acquaintance reminded me of a powerful technique called the "last three words." Here's how it works: when someone makes a statement, you respond by echoing their last three words, inviting them to elaborate. Paraphrasing what someone has said, asking follow-up questions, and resisting the urge to interrupt all demonstrate attentiveness. It's simple, effective, and a fantastic way to learn more about the person you're speaking with!

Asking follow-up questions is another way to keep the conversation flowing. When someone shares something interesting, dig a little more. If they mention a recent trip, you could ask, "What was the highlight of your trip?" or "What type of new foods did you check out while you were there?" These questions show that you're interested.

People can sense when you're interested and care about what they have to say. For instance, if someone talks about a challenging situation, you might say, "That sounds tough. How are you coping with it?" This shows that you care and encourages them to open up further. These interactions, though seemingly minimal, can leave a lasting impression.

Balancing sharing and listening can take time and effort. While sharing your thoughts and experiences, it is vital to make sure you also give the other person many opportunities to speak. Conversations are a two-way street. If you find yourself talking too much, pause and invite the other person to share their thoughts. This balance ensures that both parties feel heard and valued.

COMPLIMENTS AS BRIDGES TO CONNECTION AND FRIENDSHIPS

Complimenting others effectively is a subtle yet powerful tool for building quality friendships. A well-delivered compliment should always be heartfelt and focus on qualities or actions that resonate with you.

When offering a compliment, specificity is your friend. A specific compliment demonstrates that you've taken the time to notice something meaningful about the individual. For instance, rather than saying, "You're smart," try, "I'm impressed by how clearly you explained that complex idea; it helped me understand." Additionally, ensure the compliment is relevant to the context. Tailoring your words to the moment or setting makes your praise feel more natural and connected to the interaction. Compliments that align with a person's values or efforts—such as acknowledging their perseverance or creativity—can spark a more profound connection, as they often touch on aspects they take pride in.

Complimenting others is one of the simplest and most effective ways to build rapport and strengthen relationships, especially when forming new friendships or connections. A well-timed, sincere compliment boosts the other person's confidence and signals that you value and appreciate them. Instead of defaulting to generic comments, pay close attention to the other person's unique traits, actions, or choices. A kind remark about their creativity in solving a problem, sense of humor, or dedication to a project resonates far more deeply than a casual mention of appearance.

Timing and delivery are equally important when giving compliments. Compliments should feel natural and flow seamlessly within a conversation. Avoid overloading a person with praise or making it feel forced, as this can come across as insincere. Always stay neutral. Instead, focus on moments where acknowledgment feels appropriate, such as after someone shares an accomplishment, shows creativity, or helps others. For example, if a friend tells you about a recent project they've completed, complimenting their ingenuity shows you are paying attention and value their efforts. Compliments delivered in a calm, confident tone are more likely to be received positively.

Finally, remember that compliments are about the person on the receiving end, not the giver. Avoid returning the conversation to yourself after praising yourself, as this can undermine its impact. Instead, let your compliment stand alone and allow the other person to respond naturally. Ultimately, the best compliments are those rooted in truth, delivered with care, and aimed at nurturing a sense of respect.

Transitioning from small talk to better exchanges can enrich your connections and lead to impactful interactions. It can build trust, create memorable moments, and elevate long-term relationships. You can steer conversations better by asking open-ended questions, actively listening, sharing personal stories, giving compliments, and finding common ground. Reflective listening, asking follow-up questions, showing curiosity, and balancing sharing and listening are strategies to maintain engagement. These techniques will help you connect with others, making your social interactions more fulfilling.

Time to Reflect

- Why do you think people enjoy talking about themselves? How can you use this knowledge to make others feel comfortable in a conversation?
- Remember the last time you felt nervous about starting a conversation. What caused that feeling, and how could you approach it differently next time?
- Which of the icebreakers mentioned in this chapter resonates with you the most? Why do you think it would work well for you?

CHAPTER THREE

REAL TALK: CRAFTING CONNECTIONS THAT SPARK

I n an ideal setting, it would be great to imagine sitting across from someone, the conversation flowing smoothly, and feeling an easy connection. You're not just hearing their words but wholeheartedly understanding their emotions and experiences. It does not happen accidentally; it results from empathetic listening. In our tech-focused world, where distractions are endless, mastering the art of compassionate listening can transform your relationships and social experiences.

THE ART OF EMPATHETIC LISTENING

Empathetic listening goes beyond merely hearing words. It involves understanding and feeling other people's emotions. Stephen R. Covey, in his influential work, emphasizes the principle of "Seek first to understand, then to be understood." This principle lies at the heart of empathetic listening. It means listening to understand, not just responding. When you listen empathetically, you immerse yourself fully in the other person's experience, suspending your judgments and focusing entirely on their perspective.

Putting yourself in the speaker's shoes is essential for empathetic listening. Imagine feeling what they are feeling, seeing the world through their eyes. This shift in perspective allows you to connect on a deeper level. Acknowledging and validating the speaker's feelings is another critical aspect. Phrases like "I understand how you feel" or "That sounds challenging" can make the speaker feel heard and valued. Avoiding judgment and jumping to conclusions is vital. Often, we listen with a preconceived notion or an intent to respond, but empathetic listening requires an open mind and a legitimate curiosity about the other person's experience.

Empathetic listening has numerous benefits. It lays the foundation for solid relationships. When people feel understood, they are more likely to let you in. This trust enhances emotional intelligence as you become more attuned to others' emotions and more adept at navigating social interactions. Empathetic listening also improves conflict resolution skills. By understanding the underlying emotions and perspectives in a conflict, you can address the root causes and find mutually beneficial solutions.

There are several techniques you can practice becoming a better empathetic listener. Active listening is the cornerstone. This involves nodding, sustaining a solid gaze, and verbal affirmations like "I see" or "Go on" to show that you are fully engaged. Paraphrasing what the speaker has said demonstrates that you are listening and helps clarify and confirm your understanding. For instance, if a friend says, "I'm stressed about my upcoming exams," you might respond, "It sounds like you're feeling a lot of pressure right now."

Asking open-ended questions encourages elaboration and deeper conversation. Instead of yes-or-no questions, try asking questions that invite the speaker to share more. For example, "Can you tell me more about what's been stressing you out?" This shows that you are interested in understanding their experience. Showing empathy through verbal affirmations like "I understand" or "That must be tough" further validates the speaker's feelings and encourages them to open up more.

In summary, empathetic listening is a powerful skill that can transform social interactions. You can build trust and enhance emotional intelligence by listening to understand, putting yourself in the speaker's shoes, acknowledging their feelings, and avoiding judgment. Practicing active listening, giving reflective responses, asking open-ended questions, and showing empathy through verbal affirmations can help you become a better empathetic listener.

PRACTICAL HACKS FOR REAL CONVERSATIONS

Transitioning from small talk to authentic conversations can enhance friendships or relationships. An effective way to do this is by sharing personal stories and experiences. When you share about your life, it invites others to do the same. For instance, if someone mentions they have been stressed at work, you might share a similar experience and how you managed it. This makes the conversation more engaging and shows vulnerability, which encourages reciprocity. Sharing personal stories makes interactions richer and helps build a sense of closeness.

Finding shared interests is good strategy for improving conversations. As discussed in the previous chapter, discovering mutually enjoyable activities provides a natural segue into more meaningful dialogue. For example, if you both enjoy hiking, you can discuss your favorite trails and memorable hikes or plan a future adventure together. Shared interests create a foundation for ongoing conversations and activities, making it easier to transition to deeper topics. It's through these shared passions that friendships often blossom and grow stronger.

Vulnerability plays a role in building friendships. Being open and slightly exposed can strengthen relationships by building trust and intimacy. Sharing personal challenges and triumphs allows others to see your true self, making the connection authentic. When you express your real feelings and emotions, it encourages others to do the same. This mutual vulnerability creates a sense of solidarity and understanding. For instance, sharing a difficult period in your life and how you overcame it can inspire others to open up about their struggles, intensifying the tie between you.

Attending events can be fun. Shared experiences create lasting memories and give you something to talk about. Whether it's a music concert, an art exhibit, or a personal development workshop, these events provide opportunities for meaningful interaction. Volunteering for a cause you care about is another powerful way to build a connection. Working together towards a common goal fosters a sense of teamwork and shared purpose.

Planning regular catchups ensures that you maintain and strengthen the friendship. Consistent interaction is key to building a solid relationship. Whether it's a weekly coffee date, a monthly game night, or a quarterly hiking trip, regular meetups provide opportunities for ongoing conversations and shared experiences. These meet-ups also show that you value the friendship and are willing to invest time in it.

CHARISMA AND LIKABILITY

Charisma can seem daunting for those who are shy or introverted. I know it is a trait I grapple with often. The essence of charisma—a blend of behaviors and traits that make someone compelling and likable. The excellent news is that charisma isn't an innate quality reserved for a select few. It's a learnable skill that you can develop and refine.

Behaviors You Can Adopt Today to Unlock Your Charm

Charismatic behaviors are actions and traits that make individuals engaging and attractive in social interactions. These actions are practical because they combine warmth with competence, creating a balance that draws people in. Warmth makes you approachable and likable. It signals that you are friendly and empathetic. Another power trait is competence. And it demonstrates that you are capable and knowledgeable. These traits make you relatable and respectable, an incredibly appealing combination.

Another critical aspect of charisma is creating a sense of presence and engagement. Presence means being fully in the moment and giving your full attention to the people you are with. This level of engagement is rare in today's distracted world, making it incredibly powerful. Confidence attracts people because it shows that you believe in yourself. However, too much confidence can come across as arrogance. Humility tempers this by showing that you respect and value others' contributions. This balance makes you both strong and approachable.

Practice is essential to developing and refining charismatic behaviors. Being a great listener can significantly enhance your charisma. Demonstrating heartfelt interest makes people feel understood, enhancing your charisma.

The power of storytelling is another essential element of charisma. Compelling storytelling can captivate an audience and make you more engaging. A well-structured story has a clear beginning, middle, and end. The beginning sets the context, the middle builds tension or conflict, and the end provides resolution. Using vivid imagery and emotional appeal can make your stories more relatable and memorable. For instance, instead of simply saying, "I had a challenging day at work," you might say, "Today felt like a rollercoaster. When I thought I had everything under control, a new challenge popped up, testing my patience and creativity." Incorporating personal anecdotes and experiences makes your stories authentic and relatable. People connect with real, human experiences, making your stories more impactful. Engaging the audience with relatable content ensures that your stories resonate. Find common ground with your audience and tailor your stories to their experiences and interests.

Note any habits that detract from your charisma and improve them. You can develop and refine the charismatic behaviors that make you more engaging and likable. This skill set will enhance your social interactions, making you more confident and effective in connecting with others.

BUILDING A MAGNETIC PERSONALITY

When you think of someone with a magnetic personality, you're likely picturing someone who is effortlessly likable and attracts others naturally. This allure isn't something you're born with; it's a set of traits you can learn. Authenticity and genuineness are at the heart of a magnetic personality. People are drawn to those who are real and transparent. When you're true to yourself and don't try to be someone you're not, it creates a sense of magnetism. Authenticity means showing your true feelings and thoughts, even if they make you vulnerable. This openness invites others to be themselves around you.

Confidence without arrogance is another cornerstone. Confidence shows you believe in yourself and your abilities, but it becomes a double-edged sword when it turns into conceit. Confidence should be quiet and understated, not loud and boastful. It's about knowing your worth without needing to prove it to others constantly. This balanced confidence makes you approachable and respected. Empathy and understanding further enhance your likability. When you can put yourself in someone else's shoes, it creates a strong attachment. People feel valued and understood, which draws them closer to you.

Being curious is one of the easiest ways to build real connections. When you are interested in someone's life, thoughts, or experiences, you naturally draw them in. Think of it like exploring a new story; you ask questions, listen closely, and discover what makes each person unique. The more curiosity you bring to your conversations, the easier it becomes to create friendships that grow quickly over time.

Embracing and feeling at ease with who you are is key to developing these traits. Start with self-awareness: Take time to reflect on your strengths and weaknesses. Knowing what you are good at and where you need improvement helps you navigate social interactions more effectively. Embracing authenticity means accepting yourself as you are, even your flaws. It's about being authentic in your interactions and not pretending to be someone you're not. This can help you become more relatable.

Seeking feedback from the people in your life can provide valuable insights. Sometimes, we have blind spots that others can see more clearly. Constructive feedback helps you grow and improve, contributing to your self-awareness. Engaging in personal growth is a continuous process. Whether learning new skills, reading self-help books, or attending classes, personal development enhances your confidence and competence, making you more magnetic.

Demonstrating consistency in your words and actions also builds credibility. People know they can count on you, which strengthens your relationship. Engaging in positive self-talk boosts your confidence. Remind yourself of your strengths and achievements. This positive reinforcement helps you approach social interactions with a confident mindset.

These traits and actions contribute to a magnetic personality. Focusing on authenticity, confidence, empathy, optimism, and self-awareness can help you develop a magnetic appeal that enhances your social interactions.

As you continue to explore these concepts, remember that building a magnetic personality is a journey of self-discovery and growth.

ADJUST YOUR TONE AND PACE WHEN TALKING TO PEOPLE

To say that "tone" in a conversation is vital would be a vast under-statement. I have worked with several people with the worst tone in various situations. A person who leads with a non-collaborative tone is very uncomfortable. Communication, while second nature to us, is a subtle art that evolves and requires constant fine-tuning. Many conversations happen behind screens or through brief in-person exchanges; it's easy to overlook the impact of something as funda-mental yet transformative as tone. Tone is that invisible and flows seamlessly through every word, coloring not just what we say but how it's received. Think about your last conversation—whether with your best friend, neighbor, stranger on the subway, or cousin. Did you adjust your tone for each person? If not, there is a chance you missed an opportunity to convey empathy.

Adapting tone is more than a mere social grace; it's a skill. Believe it! It's the difference between being understood and dismissed, sparking a meaningful connection, and watching an interaction fizzle. For young adults especially, adjusting tone can feel like unfamiliar terri-tory. We might think, "This is who I am; why should I have to change?" But consider this: adjusting your tone doesn't compromise your identity but empowers you to navigate the myriad personalities and contexts life throws your way. It's a nuanced skill that says, "I see you; I hear you, and I'm choosing to meet you where you are." So, let's delve into why adjusting your tone matters, the pitfalls of ignoring this skill, and how to master it without losing authenticity.

The Power of Tone: Why It Matters

Tone goes beyond just raising or lowering the pitch of your voice. It encompasses everything—volume, speed, inflection, and the words you choose to emphasize. Tone is a silent messenger; it conveys your emotional intent. A well-adjusted tone can make someone feel valued and understood, while a poorly chosen one can leave a lasting impression, often not what we intended. In reality, people don't only hear what we say; they interpret how we say it. When tone doesn't match our message, we risk appearing insincere, unkind, or even clueless. Think before you speak, and ensure your tone is how you intend it to be.

Missteps and Misunderstandings: The Risks of Ignoring Tone

The pitfalls of overlooking tone are far-reaching. Misunderstandings hurt feelings, lost opportunities, and even damaged relationships can all result from a mismatch between tone and message. Have you ever been told, "It's not what you said, but how you said it"? That statement speaks volumes. When our tone does not align with our intention, we lose control of our message. The receiver, whether consciously or subconsciously, is left to guess our true intentions, and often, they assume the worst.

Take texting, a mode of communication notorious for its tonal ambiguity. A simple "sure" can mean anything from a straightforward agreement to passive-aggressive frustration, depending on context. When we fail to adjust our tone—or provide clarity when tone is hard to convey—we leave the door open for misinterpretation. Missteps in tone can be especially harmful in relationships with people who may not know us well enough to give us the benefit of the doubt. Friends might shrug off a misplaced tone, but a new colleague, acquaintance, or family member might read far more into it.

In more serious contexts, such as work or school, a poorly adjusted tone can even jeopardize our reputations. A sharp response in a meeting or an overly casual tone in a professional email can lead others to view us as unprofessional or disrespectful. Once we gain a reputation for poor communication, it can be hard to shake, especially if people believe it's part of our personality rather than a one-time slip-up. Adjusting our tone appropriately can prevent such misunderstandings and project our true intentions more accurately. It really works!

Building the Skill: How to Master Tone Adjustment

Adjusting your tone does not come naturally to everyone, and that's okay. Like any skill, it requires self-awareness, observation, and practice. First, consider your listener. Are they close friends or strangers? Are they older, younger, or around the same age? Are they having a good day or a difficult one? While you can't know everything about a person's mood or mindset, attention to cues such as body language, facial expressions, and past interactions can help guide your approach.

Start by practicing tone adjustment in safe environments, like with friends or family members who know you well. Notice how your tone shifts when you speak with different people. How do you talk to a younger sibling compared to a professor? Once you know the adjustments you're making, you'll have a better foundation to work.

A good rule of thumb is to aim for a friendly but formal tone in professional settings. Over time, you can gauge if you can relax a bit, but it's usually better to start on the side of caution. If in doubt, mirroring can be helpful. For example, if your boss has a warm, relaxed tone, you don't need to be overly stiff in response. Instead, mirror their openness to the extent that they still feel comfortable.

It is also helpful to pause and reflect on your tone before diving into potentially sensitive conversations. When emotions run high, tone can be challenging to control, but pausing can help you collect yourself and choose words that reflect your true intentions. Practice saying what you want to say aloud in private, adjusting your tone until it feels right. Sometimes, hearing your words outside of your head can reveal whether your intended tone is coming across.

STRIKING THE BALANCE: AUTHENTICITY AND FLEXIBILITY

One of the biggest fears about adjusting tone is that we will come off as "fake" or "inauthentic." However, adapting tone isn't about pretending to be someone you're not; it's about making your message as effective as possible. Think of it as tailoring a suit—you're still you underneath, but the clothes are adjusted to fit the occasion.

Authenticity and tone adjustment can coexist. In fact, they work best together. The key is not to overdo it or make adjustments that feel unnatural. Don't force yourself to adopt a bubbly tone if you're naturally reserved, as it may appear disingenuous. Instead, focus on softening or sharpening your natural tone as needed. Authentic tone adjustment means finding the balance between who you are and your listener and then meeting somewhere in the middle.

It's also important to note that adjusting your tone doesn't mean adjusting your beliefs or values. You're not compromising your identity by changing your delivery. Instead, you're giving your thoughts the best possible chance to resonate. For instance, let's say you feel strongly about a particular issue and want to persuade someone with an opposing view. Approaching them with respect and an open tone isn't a betrayal of your beliefs; it's a strategic choice that makes them more likely to listen.

Tone as a Bridge: Cultivating Empathy and Connection

Ultimately, adjusting your tone is about building bridges rather than walls. It's an act of empathy that recognizes each person's unique perspective and respects that communication isn't a one-size-fits-all affair. In a world that often feels divided, tone adjustment can help us connect across differences.

Consider it an invitation to move beyond yourself and engage with others. By adjusting your tone, you're signaling, "I respect your perspective, and I'm willing to meet you halfway." This doesn't mean compromising your stance but instead fostering an environment where both parties feel safe sharing, listening, and growing.

Over time, you may find that adjusting your tone becomes second nature, an unconscious act of respect and understanding that enhances your relationships. As you grow and change, your ability to adapt your tone will evolve, helping you connect more profoundly and meaningfully with a wider range of people. Tone adjustment is, in many ways, a lifelong journey. Embracing it now sets you on a path for better conversations and a more prosperous, connected life.

The next time you find yourself in a conversation, take a moment to consider how your tone is coming across. Ask yourself: Am I matching my message? Am I listening, not just with my ears but with my tone? Remember, the right tone doesn't just change a conversation; it can change a relationship and, sometimes, even a life.

Have you ever been in a situation where you said the right words, but somehow, the message did not land as you intended? That's because words alone often aren't enough. Think about the tone of your voice and the pace of your talk. Imagine attending a meeting where the presenter speaks monotonously and rushes through the material. You would likely find it hard to stay engaged, and the information might not stick. Conversely, a friend who enthusiastically shares a story and well-placed pauses can draw you in effortlessly. Tone conveys emotions and intentions, setting the mood and atmosphere of the conversation. A warm and friendly tone can make casual conversations more inviting, while a firm and authoritative tone is effective in professional settings. Adjusting your tone to convey empathy and support can be effective in sensitive discussions. Practicing varying tones to match different scenarios helps ensure your message aligns with the context.

Speaking pace is another critical aspect of communication. Speaking slowly to emphasize important points allows your listeners to absorb and reflect on what you're saying. Strategically placed pauses can give your audience time to process information, making your message more precise and impactful. Adjusting your pace to match your audience's comfort level ensures they stay engaged without feeling rushed or bored. Varying your pace can maintain interest and avoid monotony, keeping your listeners attentive and involved.

Engaging in conversational practice focusing on varying pace is another effective exercise. During casual conversations, consciously slow down when discussing critical points and speed up when sharing lighter, more exciting details. This variation keeps the conversation dynamic and interesting. Participating in public speaking groups, like Toastmasters, can provide opportunities to receive feedback on your delivery. Constructive criticism from others can help you identify and target specific areas for improvement. I adored my almost four years in Toastmasters, and it was indeed one of the best things I ever did for myself!

The importance of tone and pace cannot be overstated. The unspoken elements breathe life into your words, making communication more effective and engaging. Whether in a casual conversation, a professional setting, or a sensitive discussion, mastering the subtleties of tone and pace can significantly enhance your ability to connect with others and convey your message. These skills, combined with effective eye contact, form the foundation of powerful nonverbal communication, setting you on the path to becoming a more confident and effective communicator.

You'll navigate social interactions with greater ease and confidence by honing these skills. As we move forward, we'll explore how these nonverbal cues create a cohesive and compelling communication style, enhancing your ability to connect with others meaningfully.

Time to Reflect

- When was the last time you felt connected in a conversation?
- Have you ever stopped seeing things from someone else's point of view?
- How might imagining yourself in their shoes have changed how the conversation went?

- Do you catch yourself jumping to conclusions while someone's talking?
- What can you do to stay open-minded and curious when you're listening?
- Is there someone in your life you wish you were closer to?

Your Voice Matters

If my book sparked a new idea, inspired you, or even kept you in good company for a while, I'd love to hear your thoughts.

Honest reviews help other readers decide if this book is what they need, and your voice can make all the difference!

Leaving a review only takes a moment!

Thank you for supporting this empowerment mission.

Scan the QR code with your smartphone camera below to leave your review:

Or Use the Link: https://www.amazon.com/review/create-review/?asin=1966339003

With heartfelt thanks,
René Clayton

CHAPTER FOUR

EMOTIONAL INTELLIGENCE TODAY: THE EMOJI ISN'T ALWAYS THE MESSAGE

There's this unwritten rule of digital life: no matter how many words we type, send, or screenshot, communication in the digital age remains an art—and sometimes, a complete mess. We live in a world where the thumbs-up emoji can spark debates, where a period at the end of a text feels passive-aggressive, and where "seen" can either mean *I'm busy* or *I'm ignoring you forever.*

But here's the deal: as wild as it all seems, navigating these moments doesn't have to be impossible. Emotional intelligence (EI) is the ability to understand, manage, and respond to emotions, has always been crucial for human connection. It's just that now, we're applying it to DMs, TikTok comments, and voice memos. And trust me, it's not as intimidating as it sounds.

This chapter is your guide to learning emotional intelligence in the digital age, so you can handle any conversation—whether it's online, offline, or somewhere in between—with ease. We'll dive into the why and the how, with a healthy dose of humor to keep things real. After all, if you can't laugh at yourself when you accidentally leave someone on "read," are you even human?

THE SOCIAL MAZE: HOW WE GOT HERE

Think about this: it's 1995. Your parents are chatting on landlines, leaving awkward voicemails, or writing actual letters. Every interaction had a clear rhythm: you spoke, they spoke, and body language filled in the gaps. Fast forward to now, and the game has completely changed. We're no longer just interpreting raised eyebrows or funny faces; we're decoding a symphony of text, subtext, emojis, and memes.

And it's not just that we've moved online; it's that the *rules* keep changing. A few years ago, double texting (sending a second text before getting a reply) was a mistake. Now, it's practically encouraged. Leaving a period at the end of a sentence used to be expected, but today, it screams, "I'm upset" or "We're done here." The result? A swirling mix of confusion, second-guessing, and, let's be honest, many accidental misunderstandings.

But don't worry; emotional intelligence is here to save the day. It's the skill that helps you read between the lines, understand people's emotions (even when hidden behind a screen), and respond in ways that build trust and make interactions smoother.

THE POWER OF EMOTIONAL INTELLIGENCE WITH SELF-AWARENESS IN YOUR CONVERSATIONS

Something is captivating about people who effortlessly navigate conversations, leaving others feeling seen, understood, and valued. These individuals aren't born with a unique gift; they've refined two powerful skills: self-awareness and emotional intelligence. These traits are not reserved for motivational speakers or CEOs—they're accessible to everyone and can profoundly transform how we interact with the world.

SELF-AWARENESS IS YOUR EDGE

Let's start with the most important person in your life: you. Self-awareness is the foundation of emotional intelligence, and it's what allows you to recognize your own feelings before they spiral into a full-blown drama.

Think about the last time you got a text that made your stomach drop. Maybe it was a "we need to talk" or a simple "hey." Your brain likely went into overdrive: *What did I do wrong? Are they mad?* But here's the truth: their message is neutral. Your *reaction*—that wave of anxiety—comes from something inside you. Maybe it's fear of conflict, insecurity about the relationship, or just a bad mood from spilling coffee on your shirt that morning.

Recognizing your emotions before they hijack your brain is like hitting pause on a chaotic playlist. When you feel triggered, ask yourself: *Why am I feeling this way?* Is it about the message—or something else? Often, the answer lies in your patterns and experiences. And once you identify that, you're already halfway to resolving it.

Discovering Your Social GPS

You know that feeling when your phone's GPS suddenly starts working after being stuck on "recalculating" for what feels like forever? That moment of clarity when you finally know exactly where you are and where you're heading? That is what self-awareness does for your social life. It's like having an emotional GPS that helps you navigate every conversation, relationship, and social situation.

Self-awareness is the cornerstone of effective communication. It's recognizing and understanding your emotions, thoughts, and behaviors in real-time. This awareness allows you to present yourself authentically while staying tuned into how you come across to others. Conversations flow better when you're mindful of your tone, body language, and even the emotional energy you bring to the interaction. It helps you strike a balance—confident but not overbearing, attentive but not overzealous.

The Three-Second Rule

Self-awareness also keeps you present in the moment. It's easy to let your mind wander during a conversation or to focus so much on what you'll say next that you miss the nuances of what's being said. Grounding yourself in the present moment allows you to truly engage, making the interaction more meaningful. Furthermore, self-awareness acts as a protective mechanism against conversational pitfalls. The internal editor catches you before you interrupt, over-share, or say something you might regret.

Here's a great technique "The Three-Second Rule". The next time you feel an emotional reaction to something – anything – pause for just three seconds. In those three seconds, ask yourself:

- What am I feeling right now?
- Where do I feel it in my body?
- What triggered this feeling?

It sounds simple, right? But this tiny habit can revolutionize your social awareness. It's like installing a super-sensitive emotional radar system in your brain.

The Mirror Effect

Have you ever met someone who can read the room like a bestseller? They sense the mood before it's even spoken—knowing exactly when to lighten things up, when to stay serious, or when to simply listen. It's not luck, and it's definitely not magic. It's called social mirroring, a skill rooted in one essential practice: self-awareness.

Think of yourself as a mirror. If your surface is cloudy with your own emotional clutter, how can you possibly reflect others clearly? To truly connect, you first need to clean the mirror—acknowledge your own emotions, clear the noise, and center yourself. Only then can you reflect the world around you with clarity and precision.

The Emotional Weather Report

Self-awareness can be your best superpower, starting by tuning in to your emotions. Before entering any social scene, pause and ask yourself: "What am I feeling right now?" This quick check-in boosts your confidence and sets you up for impactful connections. Whether it's nervousness, excitement, or even fatigue, naming your emotions helps you manage them effectively. This practice prevents your mood from unconsciously dictating how you interact. Self-awareness also means listening to your inner narrative, the story you tell yourself about who you are in social settings. Negative self-talk, like "I'm terrible at small talk," can sabotage your confidence. Reframing these thoughts into positive affirmations, such as "I'm curious to learn about others," can set the stage for a more successful interaction.

While self-awareness is the foundation of great conversations, emotional intelligence builds the structure. Emotional intelligence is the ability to understand and manage your emotions while recognizing and responding to the emotions of others. This skill transforms surface-level interactions into deeper connections. At its core, EI allows you to step into someone else's shoes, encouraging empathy and consideration.

Every morning, give yourself an emotional weather report as a daily exercise. Are you feeling sunny and energetic? Cloudy with a chance of anxiety? Stormy and irritable? Understanding your own emotional weather helps you:

- Predict how you might react in different situations.
- Adjust your communication style accordingly.
- Set appropriate boundaries.
- Choose the right moments for important conversations.

The Authenticity Advantage

Here's something that might surprise you: the more self-aware you become, the less you'll care about crafting a perfect image. It's ironic, but true. When you really know yourself, you become more comfortable with your quirks, flaws, and unique traits.

One concept that helps me and that I have found to be a powerful application of self-awareness is choosing and keeping lasting friendships. Think of self-awareness as your friendship filter—it helps you identify which relationships truly serve you and which ones might be holding you back.

The Communication Compass

Self-awareness isn't just about understanding your feelings – it's also about recognizing your communication patterns. Similarly, practicing mindfulness—focusing fully on the present moment—can sharpen your awareness. Whether it's noticing the tone of someone's voice or the words they emphasize, mindfulness enhances your ability to stay engaged.

Are you someone who:

- Tends to interrupt others when excited?
- Uses humor to deflect serious conversations?
- Overanalyzes text messages before sending?

Knowing these patterns doesn't mean you need to change them all. Sometimes, these quirks make you uniquely you. The goal is to be aware of them so you can adjust when necessary.

Your Self-Awareness Journey

As we wrap up this chapter, remember that self-awareness is a journey, not a destination. It's about progress, not perfection. Each interaction, each conversation, and each social media scroll is an opportunity to learn more about yourself and how you relate to others.

Your homework? Start small. Choose one technique from this chapter – maybe it's the Three-Second Rule or the Emotional Weather Report. Practice it for a week. Notice what changes. Then, when you're ready, add another tool to your self-awareness toolkit.

At their core, these skills are about connection. When you cultivate self-awareness, you gain insight into how you show up in the world. When you develop emotional intelligence, you unlock the ability to understand and empathize with others. Together, they create the foundation for authentic, meaningful relationships. Whether you're building new friendships, mending old ones, or simply striving to be a better communicator, these traits empower you to make every interaction count.

Remember, in a world that's constantly trying to shape you into something else, the greatest power you have is knowing who you truly are. Take the time to know yourself, listen to others, and embrace the transformative power of these skills. The world is waiting for the connections only you can create.

EMPATHY IN THE DIGITAL WORLD

Empathy is often called the heart of emotional intelligence—and for good reasons. It's the ability to understand and share someone else's feelings. But in the digital age, empathy has to work overtime. Why? Because you're not just interpreting words; you're piecing together clues from context, timing, and tone (or lack thereof).

Here's an example. Your friend texts you, "I'm fine," after a fight. Technically, "I'm fine" means they're okay. But you and I both know that's rarely the case. So, what do you do? Instead of taking their words at face value, you lean into empathy. You think about their tone, their personality, and the situation. Maybe "I'm fine" really means *I'm upset, but I don't know how to talk about it.*

Empathy isn't about being a mind reader; it's about being curious. Instead of jumping to conclusions, ask questions. "Are you sure you're alright? I'm here if you want to talk." This approach opens doors rather than shutting them. And remember: sometimes, people need time. Being empathetic doesn't mean solving their problems on the spot—it means letting them know you care.

The Language of Connection

One of the larger challenges in digital communication is that words on a screen can feel cold or unclear. That's where the "language of connection" comes in minor tweaks that make your messages more thoughtful and human.

Take emojis, for example. They're like emotional punctuation marks, adding warmth and nuance to your words. A simple "thanks" feels polite but distant. Add a 😊 or 🙌, and suddenly it's friendly and enthusiastic. But here's the catch: don't rely too heavily on emojis to do the heavy lifting. If you're apologizing or expressing something serious, words still matter most.

Another tip? Be clear. We can rely on tone and body language to clarify what we mean in real life. Online, you don't have that luxury. So instead of saying, "Whatever works," try, "I'm happy with either option—let me know what you prefer!" Clarity shows respect and prevents unnecessary back-and-forth.

And for the love of Wi-Fi, don't leave people on "read" if you can help it. A quick "Got it!" or "I'll reply later" goes a long way in keeping the conversation alive and showing that you value the other person's time.

Repair, Don't Flee

Even with the best intentions, mistakes happen. You sent a snarky reply you didn't mean. You forget to respond to an important text. You misinterpret someone's tone and overreact. Guess what? That's okay. Emotional intelligence isn't about being perfect; it's about how you handle imperfection.

When things go wrong, don't ghost or double down. Instead, lean into repair. A simple apology—"Hey, I'm sorry if my last message came off wrong. I didn't mean it that way"—can diffuse almost any tension. It shows maturity, accountability, and a willingness to grow. And here's the secret: most people are far more forgiving than you think.

The Big Picture: Emotional Intelligence for Thriving in a Digital Landscape

At its core, emotional intelligence is about connection. It's about seeing humanity behind the screen—the friend who needs encouragement, the stranger who's having a bad day, the family member who misses you but doesn't know how to say it. In an increasingly digital world, emotional intelligence is the bridge that keeps us very human.

Embracing emotional intelligence in our digital lives isn't just a skill —it's a pathway to deeper connections and more meaningful interactions. By staying aware of your emotions and those of others, you can confidently navigate this ever-evolving world.

So, take a deep breath the next time you're staring at a blinking cursor or a message notification. Remember that every interaction is an opportunity—not just to communicate but to connect. And if all else fails? Send a GIF of a puppy. Trust me, it works every time.

Time to Reflect and Exercises

The Emotional Intelligence Toolkit

Let's build your emotional intelligence toolkit with some practical exercises:

The Reality Check List

Ask yourself these questions regularly:

- Am I trying to be someone I'm not in certain situations?

- Are my reactions genuine, or am I performing for others?
- Do I feel energized or drained after social interactions?

The Energy Exchange Theory

Every interaction involves an exchange of energy. After spending time with someone, ask yourself:

- Do I feel energized or drained?
- Was I able to be my authentic self?
- Did the conversation flow naturally or feel forced?
- Would I look forward to seeing this person again?

Pause Practice

- Before responding to any message or comment that triggers you, take a deep breath.
- Count to five.
- Ask yourself if your reaction is coming from a place of clarity or emotion.

The Body Scan

- Set a daily reminder.
- Take 30 seconds to notice physical sensations.
- Connect these sensations to your emotional state.

The Future You Foundation

Self-awareness isn't just about understanding who you are now – it's about shaping who you want to become.

Consider:

- How do you want others to feel in your presence?
- What kind of energy do you want to bring to conversations?
- How can you use your understanding of yourself to impact others positively?

The Growth Mindset Gateway

Remember, self-awareness isn't about harsh self-judgment – it's about growth and understanding. Think of it as your personal development superpower.

The more you understand yourself:

- The better you can convey your needs.
- The more authentic your relationships become.
- The easier it is to navigate social situations.
- The more confident you feel in your own skin.

CHAPTER FIVE

THE COURAGE TO CONNECT: WHY AND HOW TO MAKE NEW FRIENDS IN THE DIGITAL AGE

In the time of many video calls that let us connect across continents, one would think that making new friends would be more accessible than ever. Yet, for many, the tools designed to unite us often leave us feeling more isolated and unsure of how to connect with others. Young adults frequently search for new friendships but may find developing deep, intimate connections challenging.

Making new friends isn't just a nice-to-have—it's a must-have for our emotional and physical well-being. And the good news? With a little courage, intentionality, and vulnerability, we can create new connections that enrich our lives, no matter where we are or what stage of life we're in.

THE SCIENCE OF FRIENDSHIP: WHY IT MATTERS

Before we dive into the "how," let's ground ourselves in the true "why." Friendship isn't just a social luxury; it's a fundamental part of our health and happiness. Research has consistently shown that having close relationships can:

- **Increase physical health**: A strong social network has been linked to reduced stress and even a longer lifespan.
- **Enhance mental well-being**: Friendships provide emotional support during rough times, reduce the risk of depression, and foster a sense of belonging.
- **Improve resilience**: When we face life's challenges, friends can help us bounce back by offering perspective and encouragement.

Loneliness, on the other hand, has been dubbed an epidemic, with health effects comparable to smoking fifteen cigarettes a day. The stakes couldn't be higher. The absence of connection doesn't just make us sad—it can make us very ill.

WHY IS IT SO HARD TO MAKE FRIENDS AS ADULTS?

Think back to childhood or college; those were the main friendship years. Proximity and shared experiences (like gym class or late-night study sessions) created fruitful ground for connection. As adults, though, we lose those built-in opportunities. Add in busy schedules, family commitments, and the rise of digital communication, and it's no wonder making new friends feels daunting.

Some common barriers include:

1. **Fear of rejection**: It's vulnerable to put yourself out there and risk someone not reciprocating your desire for connection.
2. **Lack of time**: Between work, family, and personal chores, carving out time for new friendships can feel pretty much impossible.

3. **The illusion of digital connection**: Social media can trick us into feeling connected, but liking someone's Instagram post isn't the same as knowing them.
4. **Difficulty breaking into groups**: Many people already have their "core" group, and it can feel intimidating to join in.

These barriers aren't insurmountable. Making new friends might initially feel awkward, but it's also rewarding.

The significance of friendships for young adults, especially those who are single, cannot be overstated. A recent study published in *PLOS ONE* sheds light on how these relationships profoundly influence happiness and overall well-being among individuals aged 18 to 24.

THE STUDY AT A GLANCE

Researchers from the University of California, Los Angeles, analyzed data from 1,073 single young adults. They assessed participants' happiness levels alongside five key predictors: satisfaction with family, satisfaction with friends, self-esteem, neuroticism, and extraversion. Using latent profile analysis, they identified five distinct subgroups, each exhibiting unique combinations of these predictors and corresponding happiness levels.

Key Findings

The study revealed that satisfaction with friendships emerged as a particularly strong factor for well-being in young, single adults. Those most satisfied with their friendships were happiest, while those least satisfied showed lower happiness.

Implications for Young Adults

These findings underscore the importance of cultivating meaningful friendships during emerging adulthood. As many young adults navigate life without long-term romantic partners, friendships provide essential support, companionship, and a sense of belonging. Deliberately fostering and maintaining these relationships can significantly enhance happiness and overall life satisfaction.

Practical Steps to Enhance Friendships

- **Invest Time and Effort:** Prioritize spending quality time with friends, whether through shared activities, regular catch-ups, or simply being present during challenging times.
- **Communicate Openly:** Honest and open communication strengthens trust and deepens connections.
- **Be Supportive:** Offer support and encouragement, celebrate successes, and provide comfort during setbacks.
- **Stay Connected:** In today's digital age, utilize technology to maintain connections, especially when physical meet-ups aren't feasible.

Friendships play a pivotal role in the happiness and well-being of single young adults. By actively nurturing these relationships, individuals can create a robust support system that enriches their lives and contributes to lasting happiness.

THE "HOW" - NEW FRIENDS IN THE DIGITAL AGE

1. Mindset Shift

The initial step to developing new connections is believing it's worth it—and knowing it's possible. Making friends isn't just about luck or chemistry; it's a skill that can be cultivated. Shift your mindset from "I'm not great at this" to "I know I can definitely do this! " Approach new friendships with courage, knowing that each interaction is an opportunity to connect, no matter how small.

2. Be Deliberate About Where You Look

While friendships can sometimes form organically, you're more likely to make friends by being proactive. Here's how:

- **Reconnect with old acquaintances**: Rekindling relationships with people you already know but have lost touch with is often the key to forming new friendships.
- **Leverage your existing network**: Ask friends, family, or coworkers to introduce you to people with similar interests. The best connections are just one degree away.
- **Join communities**: One of the easiest ways to meet like-minded individuals is to engage in shared activities, such as a sports club, a yoga class, or a social media group for people who share your passions.

3. Take It Offline if It is Safe

Digital platforms are a great starting point, but an IRL connection happens when you go past the screen. If you meet someone online, suggest an in-person meetup or a video call. This is where the relationship moves from basic to meaningful.

- **Say yes to invitations**: Even if you feel unsure, accepting invitations to events or gatherings is crucial to meeting new people.
- **Host gatherings**: Whether it's a pizza night, a game day, or a forest hike, creating opportunities for people to come together can help nurture new friendships.

4. Embrace Vulnerability

Friendship thrives on authenticity. To form deep connections, you must be willing to show up as your true self—flaws, fears, and all. This doesn't mean oversharing, but it does mean going beyond small talk. Ask thoughtful questions, share your thoughts and feelings, and tell others they're valued.

Here are some questions to deepen conversations:

- What's something you're passionate about right now?
- What's a dream you're working toward?
- What's the best part of your day?

5. Consistency Is Key

Friendships aren't built overnight. They require time, energy, and repeated interactions to grow. Make a point of regularly checking in with new connections, whether it's through a quick text, a coffee date, or a phone call. Consistency signals to others that you value the relationship and are invested in its growth.

6. Set Boundaries with Technology

Digital tools can enhance friendships, but they can also hinder them. Be mindful of how you use technology. For example:

- Use social media to facilitate real-world connections, not replace them.
- Schedule screen-free time to focus on in-person interactions.
- Avoid falling into the trap of passive engagement (e.g., mindlessly liking posts) and prioritize active communication (e.g., direct messages or video calls).

The Courage to Keep Trying

Perhaps the most critical ingredient in making new friends is resilience. Not every attempt will lead to a deep connection, and that's okay. Instead of viewing unsuccessful attempts as failures, see them as steps toward finding the right people. Friendship, like any meaningful endeavor, requires persistence.

Let's not forget the power of showing up. In a world where so many of us feel unseen, being present and genuinely interested in others can make a profound difference. Be the person who reaches out, listens, and takes the first step—even when it feels uncomfortable.

Friendship Is a Lifelong Practice

Making new friends in the digital age isn't just about expanding your social circle; it's about cultivating connections that help you thrive. It's about embracing vulnerability, showing up authentically, and being willing to take risks for the sake of connection.

As we navigate this ever-changing landscape of technology and human interaction, remember that the tools we use don't define our friendships. We do. And when we approach connection with courage, curiosity, and intentionality, we open ourselves to the kind of relationships that enrich our lives in ways nothing else can.

So here's my challenge to you: this week, take one step—just one—toward making a new friend. Whether it's sending a nice text, attending an event, or simply smiling at a stranger, let that small act be a reminder that connection is always within reach. Because the truth is, we're wired for this. We're wired to have friends. And no matter how frightening it feels, the courage to connect is always worth it.

REAL-LIFE SUCCESS STORIES: FROM WALLFLOWER TO SOCIAL BUTTERFLY

In a scene in your mind, you step into a room full of strangers, your mind goes blank, your palms are steamy, and all you can think is, "Why did I agree to this?" Now, imagine a different version of that moment—where you walk in quickly, start conversations like a pro, and enjoy yourself, connecting with people in a natural and fun way. Seems like a stretch? Not at all. With some practice and the right mindset, you can turn that nerve-wracking scenario into one of confidence and connection.

MEET ALEX: THE COFFEEHOUSE CONQUEROR

Alex, a 20-year-old art student, used to hide behind her sketchbook in crowded cafes. Her social anxiety was her constant companion, whispering doubts and fears. But one day, she decided to flip the script.

"I started small," Alex shares. "I challenged myself to smile at one person each day. It was terrifying at first, but the rush of accomplishment was addictive!"

Alex's breakthrough came when she complimented a stranger's unique laptop sticker. "We ended up chatting for an hour about our favorite bands. I realized people are just waiting for an invitation to connect."

Now, Alex hosts weekly sketch meetups at her favorite coffeehouse. "Being authentic about my passion opened doors I never knew existed. My anxiety still pops up, but now it's more like background noise than a blaring alarm."

THE JASON TRANSFORMATION: FROM GAMER TO GAME-CHANGER

Jason, 24, was more comfortable with NPCs (non-player characters) than real people. His idea of socializing was limited to online gaming forums.

"I felt like I was speaking a different language in the real world," Jason admits. "But then I realized – I just needed to translate my online skills to offline interactions."

Jason's eureka moment? Treating social situations like a game quest. "I'd set mini-challenges for myself, like 'Initiate three conversations at this party' or 'Find out one interesting fact about each person in your study group.'"

His strategy paid off. Jason now leads a thriving local gaming community that meets online and in person. "Being real about my interests helped me find my tribe. Now I'm leveling up my social skills and helping others do the same!"

EMMA'S EMPATHY REVOLUTION

Emma, 27, always felt like an outsider until she discovered the power of active listening. "I used to obsess over what to say next, which ironically made me a terrible conversationalist," she laughs.

Her hidden talent? Focusing on others instead of herself. "I started asking open-ended questions and listening to the answers. Suddenly, people found me fascinating – all because I found them fascinating first!"

Emma's newfound skill led her to start a popular podcast in which she interviews fellow students about their passions. "Authenticity is magnetic," she says. When you're interested in others, they can't help but be drawn to you."

QUOTES TO IGNITE YOUR SOCIAL SPARK

"Embracing your quirks is the fastest way to find your people."

— *ALEX*

"Every social interaction is a chance to level up. Embrace the XP!"

— *JASON*

"Curiosity is the ultimate social lubricant. Be interested, and you'll always be interesting."

— *EMMA*

Remember, these success stories aren't about becoming someone you're not. They're about unleashing the amazing, authentic you that's been hiding behind that shield of social anxiety. Your story could be next!

PART TWO
BREAKING THE WALLS

CHAPTER SIX

CRUSH SOCIAL ANXIETY

W hen I go to new places or events, I often feel intimidated. Initially, I was even proud that I had made it to the place! However, the thought of approaching a stranger and starting a conversation can feel insurmountable. For you, it could show up as your heart racing and a voice in your head whispers, "What if they don't like me? What if I say something wrong?" This fear of rejection is a common hurdle many young adults face.

THE SOCIAL SHIFT: NAVIGATING INTERACTION

High rates of anxiety can significantly impact young adults' social lives and interactions. Social disconnection and isolation can increase the risk of various health issues, according to the American Psychological Association.

Growing up, we moved every year until I was around thirteen. It led to having to talk to new people all the time, continually having social anxiety, not knowing my classmates the way they knew each other, and so much more. While I did learn valuable skills during these moves, it was hard, especially as a child. I became an anxious and awkward person, which took years to overcome.

I put this book together to help everyone (including me!) socialize effectively, talk to anyone easily, and make new friends.

STEPS TO CONQUER SOCIAL ANXIETY

Social anxiety can be a challenging obstacle in building confidence and forming connections. It's essential first to identify what specifically triggers your anxiety in social situations. Common triggers include public speaking, meeting new people, large gatherings, and being the center of attention. Understanding these triggers can help you develop strategies to manage your anxiety effectively. I like to write these down or keep a list on my phone.

When I was a sophomore in high school, I was shy and often uneasy. We had to do a presentation in front of the class, and when my classmate and I were in the front of the room, I started to laugh uncontrollably, which made her laugh as well. It was super embarrassing. Fortunately, I had a great teacher who understood and let us try again the next day.

Public speaking is a significant trigger for many. The thought of standing in front of people, with all eyes on you, can be terrifying. Your mind races with worst-case scenarios, and your body responds with physical symptoms like sweating, shaking, and a pounding heart. Meeting new people can also be nerve-wracking. You might worry about making a good impression or fear that you'll say something awkward. Large gatherings, such as parties or networking events, can feel overwhelming due to the sheer number of people and the cacophony of conversations. Being the center of attention, whether it's during a presentation, a group discussion, or even a birthday celebration, can amplify your anxiety.

Having immediate coping strategies can be incredibly helpful in those moments when anxiety strikes. These include:

- Mindfulness
- Optimism
- Exercise
- Sleep
- Journaling
- Breathing Exercises
- Positive Self-Talk

Mindfulness and grounding techniques can help you stay present and reduce anxiety. It involves paying attention to the present moment without judgment. When you notice your anxiety rising, take a moment to observe your surroundings. Focus on the colors, textures, and sounds around you. Grounding techniques, such as the 5-4-3-2-1 method, can also be helpful. Identify five things you can see, four things you can touch, three things you can hear, two things you can smell, and one thing you can taste. These exercises help shift your focus away from anxious thoughts and into the present moment. For example, I think or say to myself, "the air is cold and breezy on my skin", or "this shirt feels soft and clean", etc.

Positive visualization is another powerful tool. Before entering a social setting, take a few minutes to visualize yourself confidently managing it. Picture yourself speaking, participating in conversations, and feeling the fear and doing it anyway. Visualize positive outcomes, such as receiving smiles and nods of approval. This mental rehearsal can boost your confidence and reduce anxiety.

In addition to immediate coping strategies, incorporating long-term anxiety management practices into your daily life can significantly reduce overall anxiety. Regular physical exercise is one of the most effective ways to manage anxiety. Exercise releases endorphins, which are natural mood lifters. It also reduces levels of the body's stress hormones, such as adrenaline and cortisol. Aim for at least twenty minutes of moderate exercise most days of the week. I love going to the gym or walking outside when the weather is nice. I have two dogs, so, fortunately, they keep me busy outside.

A consistent sleep schedule is another helpful tool. Lack of sleep can aggravate anxiety, so it's important to prioritize good sleep routines. Try to go to bed and wake up at the same time each day, even on weekends. The area of a consistent sleep schedule has never been easy for me. I found that keeping to a relaxed bedtime routine can signal to my body that it's time to wind down. This might include reading a book, taking a warm shower, or stretching before bed. We all know to avoid scrolling on social media and our phones before bed. I know this is a challenge most of us face, yet it is good to stay away from this habit.

Journaling is a wonderful way to track triggers and progress. Set aside a few minutes daily to write about your experiences and feelings. Note any specific situations that triggered your anxiety and how you responded. Reflecting on these entries can help you identify patterns and develop strategies for managing anxiety more effectively. Journaling also provides an outlet for expressing emotions and can be therapeutic.

Breathing exercises are one of the simplest yet most effective tools. Focusing on your breath and taking slow, deep breaths can calm your nervous system and reduce anxiety. There are a couple to practice. I like breathing in twice through my nose, then slowly out quietly through my mouth with an eight count. Or, try inhaling deeply through your nose for a count of four, holding your breath for four seconds, and then exhaling slowly through your mouth for a count of six. Repeat this a few times until you feel calmer.

Self-talk is the inner dialogue that runs through your mind, and when it comes to social anxiety, it can either be your worst enemy or your greatest ally. For many young adults, negative self-talk takes center stage before and during social interactions— "What if I say something stupid?" or "Everyone's judging me right now." These thoughts amplify anxiety, making even small conversations feel overwhelming. The key to crushing social anxiety is recognizing this pattern and actively shifting your self-talk from self-criticism to self-support. Instead of focusing on potential mistakes, practice telling yourself things like, "I'm learning to connect, and that's a win," or "I don't have to be perfect; I just have to be present." This shift can help you break free from the mental loop of doubt and fear.

Positive self-talk isn't about pretending your anxiety doesn't exist; it's about acknowledging it without letting it control you. Picture your inner dialogue as a coach instead of a critic—one that encourages you to step out of your comfort zone while offering kindness when things don't go as planned. When you remind yourself that awkward moments are normal and everyone feels unsure sometimes, you create space for growth and connection. Over time, this intentional shift in self-talk can transform how you approach social situations, making them less about potential failure and more about the opportunity to connect, grow, and enjoy the moment.

By recognizing your triggers, acting immediately with coping strategies, incorporating long-term practices, or getting help when needed, you can effectively manage social anxiety. These techniques will empower you to navigate social settings, paving the way for a fulfilling social life.

THE SHADOW OF REJECTION

The fear of rejection is significantly rooted in our evolutionary history. In ancient times, being part of a group or tribe was necessary for survival. Acceptance meant access to resources, protection, and social bonds, while rejection could lead to isolation and danger. This need for belonging has been carried over into modern society, where social acceptance still plays a part in our emotional well-being. When we perceive a threat to social acceptance, our brain triggers a response like physical pain, as shown by research in the PMC article "Emotional responses to interpersonal rejection."

Rejection elicits strong emotional reactions, including hurt feelings, embarrassment, and social anxiety. These emotions serve as signals, prompting us to pay immediate attention to the perceived threat to our social standing. For example, when we are excluded from social activity or criticized by peers, we may experience a sharp sense of hurt and shame. This emotional response is our brain's way of protecting us from further social harm. However, these feelings can hinder our willingness to engage in social interactions, creating a vicious cycle of avoidance and isolation.

To cope with rejection, reframe it as a learning opportunity rather than a personal failure. Every negative response can teach us something valuable about ourselves. We can reduce rejection's negative impact by viewing it as a chance to grow. Practicing self-compassion and positive self-talk is also a significant factor. Remember that everyone experiences rejection at some point, which doesn't define your worth.

Setting realistic expectations is another key strategy. Not every interaction will lead to a real connection or immediate acceptance. This mindset helps you approach social situations with a balanced perspective, reducing the pressure to perform perfectly. When you accept that rejection is a natural part of social interactions, it becomes less intimidating and more manageable.

Desensitization techniques can further help you become more comfortable with the possibility of rejection. Gradual exposure to social risks is an effective method. I like to start with low-stakes inter-actions, such as asking a stranger for directions or complimenting a coworker. As you build confidence, gradually take on more chal-lenging social scenarios. Role-playing rejection scenarios with a friend can also be beneficial. Practice handling different types of rejection, such as a declined invitation or a dismissive response, to prepare yourself for real-life situations.

Reflecting on past rejections and their actual impact can provide valuable insights. We often realize rejection's consequences are not as terrible as we feared. For instance, you might recall a time when you were turned down for a date. While it felt devastating at the moment, it likely did not have a lasting effect on your life. This reflection helps you put future rejections into perspective, reducing their emotional impact. I have learned through experiences that the more we can put ourselves out there in the world and try different things, learning to hear the word "no" (or not right now) will help build up that muscle, and it won't feel as heavy.

I recall early on in my career when I was nervous about presenting a new idea at a work meeting. Despite my fears, I went ahead, and while a few co-workers were critical, others appreciated my initiative. This experience (and many similar ones) taught me that there can be valuable support even in the face of rejection.

You can overcome rejection through time and experience.

TACKLING SOCIAL ANXIETY IN SPECIFIC SITUATIONS

Social anxiety in different settings can be particularly scary, affecting performance and self-esteem. Let's explore why these environments trigger anxiety and how you can manage it effectively.

Gliding Through Social Gatherings

Social gatherings can be a minefield for those prone to anxiety. Large crowds and unfamiliar faces often present immediate triggers. You walk into a loud party where everyone seems to know each other, and suddenly, you feel lost in the sea of conversations. The fear of being judged or embarrassed can quickly take hold, making it hard to relax and be yourself. The pressure to engage in small talk can be overwhelming, as you may worry about saying the wrong thing or running out of things to say. Add to this the sensory overload from noise, music, and general activity, and it's no wonder social events can be so anxiety-inducing.

When preparing for a group event, set realistic expectations and goals. Understand that you do not need to win the room or make a hundred new friends. Aiming to have a couple of meaningful conversations could be easier to digest. Wear something that makes you feel empowered, which can boost your mood and help you feel secure. If possible, arriving with a friend or neighbor can provide support and make it smoother to break into conversations. If you start feeling overwhelmed, having a pre-planned exit strategy can give you a quick way out, reducing anxiety about being trapped in an uncomfortable situation.

After the event, taking time for post-event reflection can be incredibly beneficial. Celebrate small successes and positive interactions, no matter how minor they may seem. Did you have an enjoyable conversation with someone new? Did you manage to stay for an hour when you thought you would leave after ten minutes? These are victories worth acknowledging. Reflecting on challenges is equally important. What made you uncomfortable? Were there moments when you felt particularly anxious? Understanding these triggers can help you prepare better for future events. Remind yourself that it's okay to feel anxious and that these experiences do not define you. Positive self-talk can reinforce this mindset, making it easier to approach future social gatherings with less trepidation.

Setting intentions for future social events can also be a powerful tool. For example, you might aim to initiate one conversation at the next event or stay for a set amount of time before leaving. These small, achievable goals can build your confidence over time. Remember, it's not about being perfect but about making progress. Each social event you attend is an opportunity to gain experience, enhancing your ability to connect with others.

Successfully Handle Social Awkwardness

When we're nervous, it's tempting to fill silence with words. Instead, focus on listening intently, nodding along, and responding thoughtfully. This makes people feel heard, which is always a great conversation booster!

Awkward silences often occur for several reasons, making conversations uncomfortable and stilted. One common cause is a lack of common interests. When you and the person you're speaking with don't share similar hobbies, experiences, or topics of interest, it can be challenging to keep the conversation flowing. This can lead to pauses as you search for something to discuss. A misaligned conversational pace is another factor. If one person speaks quickly while the other prefers a slower, more deliberate pace, it can create gaps in the dialogue. This mismatch can make it difficult to maintain a natural rhythm.

Social anxiety or nervousness plays a significant role in our lives. When you're anxious, your mind may go blank, leaving you struggling to think of what to say next. This anxiety can be compounded by fear, making you overly cautious about your words. Transitioning between topics can also lead to awkward silences. Shifting smoothly from one subject to another requires skill, which can result in uncomfortable pauses when done poorly. Understanding these common reasons can help you anticipate and manage awkward silences more effectively.

You can use several actionable methods to handle and fill awkward silences gracefully. Asking open-ended questions is a powerful technique. These questions encourage the other person to elaborate, providing more material for the conversation. For example, instead of asking, "Do you like your job?" you could ask, "What do you enjoy most about what you do?" This invites a more detailed response and keeps the conversation going. Making observational comments about your surroundings can also help. For instance, if you're at a new coffee shop, you might say, "I love the atmosphere. Have you been here before?" This fills the silence and provides a new topic to discuss.

Using humor to break the tension is another effective technique. A light-hearted joke or witty remark can diffuse the awkwardness and make the conversation more enjoyable. For example, if there's a sudden silence, you might say, "Well, this is a great opportunity to practice my mime skills!" This shows that you're comfortable with the silence and can turn it into a positive moment. Sharing a related story or anecdote can also bridge the gap. If the conversation lulls after discussing a recent movie, you could share a funny or interesting experience related to film. This personal touch makes the dialogue more engaging and relatable.

Being comfortable with silence is equally important. Occasional pauses are natural and can enhance conversations by providing moments for reflection. Practicing mindfulness to stay present can help you embrace these silences without panic. When a silence occurs, take a breath and focus on the present moment. This calm approach can ease tension and make it feel less awkward. Using silence as a reflection moment allows both parties to gather their thoughts. It's okay to take a beat to think about your next words. Try to acknowledge the silence without panicking. Simply smiling or maintaining a relaxed posture can signal you're comfortable, making the other person feel the same.

NAVIGATING CONVERSATIONAL TRAPS TO HELP ALLEVIATE ANXIETY

Even the most well-intentioned conversations can go awry due to common mishaps many people inadvertently fall into. Interrupting or talking over others is one of the most frequent mistakes. It disrupts the flow of conversation and makes the other person feel disrespected and unheard. No one likes to be interrupted, and this behavior can quickly derail a conversation, making it awkward and uncomfortable. Another common issue is dominating the discussion. When one person talks excessively without giving others a chance to speak, it can make the interaction feel one-sided. This often leaves others feeling disengaged and unimportant. Additionally, bringing up controversial or sensitive topics can be a major conversational mistake. Topics like politics, religion, or personal finances can quickly turn a friendly chat into a heated debate, causing discomfort and tension. Choosing topics that are safe and inclusive can help maintain a positive atmosphere. Stick to neutral subjects like hobbies, travel, or recent events unlikely to cause controversy.

But what happens if you do make a conversational misstep? Recovering quickly is vital. If you interrupt someone, apologize sincerely. A simple, "I'm sorry, I didn't mean to cut you off. Please, go ahead" can go a long way in mending the situation. If you find yourself in a discussion about a controversial topic, you could say, "Let's switch gears a bit. Have you heard about the new exhibit at the museum?" This steers the conversation to a more neutral subject and introduces an exciting topic to discuss. It can help mend the situation and show that you value their input. When a conversation stagnates, you might say, "That's interesting! By the way, have you tried any new restaurants lately?" This keeps the dialogue flowing and introduces a new, engaging topic. If someone dominates the conversation, gently interject, "I'd love to hear others' thoughts on this. What do you think, [Name]?" This gives others a chance to speak and subtly signals to the talkative person to share the floor.

Understanding and avoiding these common conversational traps allows you to navigate social interactions more smoothly. Practicing active listening, balancing talking and listening, staying aware of body language, and choosing safe topics can help you sidestep awkward moments. And if you do make a mistake, knowing how to recover gracefully can keep the conversation on track. These skills will enhance your ability to connect with others, making your social interactions more enjoyable and meaningful.

SOCIAL ANXIETY IN PROFESSIONAL SETTINGS

Professional or work settings often come with high stakes and performance pressure. You are expected to deliver results, meet deadlines, and impress colleagues and superiors. This pressure can be tremendous, especially if you fear judgment. The structured hierarchy in most workplaces adds another layer of complexity. Navigating these relationships requires tact and confidence. Public speaking and presentations, common in professional environments, can be major anxiety triggers. The thought of standing before an audience and delivering a speech can be intimidating, leading to physical symptoms like sweating, trembling, and a rapid heart rate.

Preparation is vital to managing anxiety in professional settings. Start by researching the event or meeting you will be attending. Knowing the agenda, the key players and the topics to be discussed can give you a sense of control. Practicing your key talking points and introductions can also help. This practice familiarizes you with the content and boosts your confidence. If you have a presentation, plan and rehearse it thoroughly. Arriving early to the venue allows you to acclimate to the environment, reducing last-minute jitters.

Reflecting on your experiences after an event is necessary for growth. Take time to think about the experience. What went well? What could have been better? Identifying successful interactions and areas for improvement helps you learn from each experience. Seek constructive feedback from a coworker. Their insights can provide valuable perspectives and help you refine your skills. Set specific goals for future professional interactions.

Workplaces can indeed be stressful, but with the right strategies, you can manage anxiety and perform effectively. Remember, preparation, in-the-moment techniques and post-event reflection are your allies. Each step builds your resilience and confidence, helping you manage your anxiety at work.

As we wrap up this chapter and learn to manage and crush anxiety, remember that progress isn't about being flawless; it's about taking small, consistent steps toward feeling more in control of your life. Social anxiety can sometimes feel like an insurmountable wall, but every brick you remove — whether it's saying "hi" to a classmate, attending a social gathering for a few minutes, or even just leaving the house on a tough day — is a victory worth celebrating. It's okay to feel nervous or awkward; these feelings don't define you. What matters is the courage you show by trying, even when it feels hard. Surround yourself with supportive people who understand and respect your boundaries and encourage your growth. Remember, every single person struggles with insecurities at some level, even if they don't show it. You're not alone in this, and there's no shame in reaching out for help when you need it, whether it's from a trusted friend, a family member, or a mental health professional.

Give yourself credit for your effort — it's not easy, but it's worth it. Social anxiety doesn't have to dictate your life story. By building a toolkit of strategies, like practicing mindfulness, challenging negative thoughts, and taking gradual steps out of your comfort zone, you're empowering yourself to live a life that feels fulfilling and true to who you are. Celebrate the little wins because they're the foundation of big changes. And don't be hard on yourself when setbacks happen (because they will — you're human!). Think of them as opportunities to learn and grow, not as failures.

Most importantly, treat yourself with the same kindness and patience you would a close friend. You are deserving of that grace, no matter what your inner critic might say. Life is a journey, and every step forward, no matter how small, is a step toward greater confidence and peace. You've got this; the world is better for having you in it. Keep going — your future self is cheering you on!

Time to Reflect

- What situations make you feel the most socially anxious, and what thoughts usually run through your mind in those moments?
- When was the last time you interacted positively with someone new? What made that experience feel easier or more comfortable?
- How do you typically respond to silence in a conversation?
- What could you do to use those moments as opportunities rather than feeling awkward?
- What's one small, low-pressure step you could take this week to step outside your social comfort zone?

PART THREE
SCREENS BETWEEN US

CHAPTER SEVEN

DIGITAL HARMONY: REAL RELATIONSHIPS IN AN ONLINE WORLD

The prevalence of screens in our lives means we spend more time engaging with devices than with people face-to-face. This shift can lead to declining social skills, such as reading body language and picking up on emotional cues, essential for sincere conversations. The convenience of digital communication sometimes comes at the cost of depth and understanding in our relationships.

For almost everyone, the digital age dilemma is the ability to stay focused on self-awareness in a world of constant digital distraction. Juggling multiple digital personalities, processing hundreds of micro-interactions daily, and keeping your emotions in check is a large undertaking.

This digital overwhelm can make staying in touch with our authentic selves harder. But here's where it gets interesting: you can use technology to enhance your communication rather than diminish it.

TEXTING AND ONLINE MESSAGING: BEHIND YOUR WORDS

Texting is one of the most common ways we communicate, especially for young adults. Whether it's through messaging apps, group chats, or socials, so many of our conversations happen through words on a screen. But unlike face-to-face interactions, texting strips away tone of voice, facial expressions, and body language—all the things that help convey how we feel. So, how do you make sure the "vibe" you want to project is coming through in your texts?

It's easy to underestimate the power of texting. Still, the truth is that the way you communicate through written words can set the entire tone for your relationships—whether it's with friends, family, or even professional contacts. Since the recipient can't see or hear you, every word you choose, the timing of your responses, and even the way you structure your messages matters. In fact, many misunderstandings happen when texting because it's so easy to misinterpret tone or intention. You might think you're sending a casual message, but it might come across as cold or uninterested if you're too short or abrupt. On the flip side, an overly long text with too many details might make you seem anxious or over-invested.

Imagine you text a friend, "Hey, are you coming to the new night-club tomorrow?" If they respond with a one-word answer like, "Maybe," that can feel vague or disinterested, even if they didn't mean it that way. The same question was answered with, "Yeah, maybe! I'm just figuring out my plans. You?" It feels more engaged and open, even though the word "maybe" is still there. The difference lies in the vibe created by adding more context, punctuation, or even an emoji to soften the tone.

One of the most essential aspects of texting is timing. The timing of your response can heavily influence how your message is received. If you take too long to respond, it might be interpreted as a lack of interest or effort, even if that's not the case. Of course, there's no need to reply instantly every time (we all have lives outside of our phones!), but being mindful of how long it takes you to respond can shape the other person's impression of the conversation. If it is someone you are trying to build a connection with, timely responses can show that you're engaged and interested in continuing the conversation.

As discussed in a previous chapter, the tone is another area where texting can get tricky. Since you don't have vocal inflections to rely on, the recipient has to interpret your message based on the words alone. This is where punctuation, word choice, and even emojis can play a huge role in managing the vibe of the conversation. A text that ends with a period might seem firm or final while adding an exclamation mark can make the same sentence feel more enthusiastic. For example, "See you later" sounds neutral or even a little flat, whereas "See you later!" feels more upbeat and friendly. Even something as simple as a well-placed smiley face can soften your words of the message.

One of the reasons texts are so easily misinterpreted is that they're often short and to the point, which can leave a lot of room for the other person to fill in the blanks. If your text is too vague or short, the recipient might read into it in a way you didn't intend. For example, texting someone, "We need to talk," could immediately send their mind into overdrive, thinking something's wrong. A more unmistakable message like "Hey, can we chat about something later? Nothing urgent!" helps set the tone and prevents misunderstandings. Having clarity in your texts will assist.

Another way to shift the mood in your texts is to reciprocate the person's energy when you are testing. If they're sending you long, detailed messages and you respond with one-word answers, they could feel like you're not interested in the conversation. On the flip side, if they keep things short and casual, a long-winded response might overwhelm them or make them feel out of sync. Pay attention to the rhythm of the conversation and try to keep your messages on a similar wavelength. This doesn't mean you have to mirror their style exactly, but finding a balance helps maintain a smooth, natural flow.

While text conversations can sometimes feel transactional, it's important to remember that they're still a form of connection. Adding little touches that show you're paying attention to the other person's feelings or needs can go a long way in shaping a positive impression. For example, if a friend texts you about a stressful day, simply acknowledging their emotions with something like, "That sounds tough, I hope things get better soon!" shows empathy, even if the conversation is happening through a screen.

One final thing to consider in texting is when to take the conversation offline. Texting is great for quick exchanges or staying in touch, but some conversations are better had in person or over the phone, especially when emotions are involved. If you sense that the vibe is off —maybe the conversation feels tense, or there's a misunderstanding that's hard to clear up through text—it might be best to suggest a call or Facetime. Texting can make it difficult to convey complex emotions or tones, and talking face-to-face (even virtually) allows for a more natural flow of communication where you can pick up on the other person's body language and voice.

Texting may not allow for the full range of nonverbal cues that face-to-face conversations offer, but it still has its own set of "vibes" to manage. The words you choose, the timing of your responses, and the way you structure your messages all contribute to how you're perceived. By being mindful of these factors, you can ensure that your texts send the right signals, whether keeping things light with friends or handling a more serious conversation.

BREAKING THE SOCIAL MEDIA SPELL: REDISCOVERING REAL CONNECTIONS IN A DIGITAL WORLD

Welcome to the wild, wonderful world of digital communication – where your words can make someone's day, change their mind, or at least make someone smile. I remember my first time on Facebook and Twitter (now "X"), and I think I posted about my delicious and hot morning coffee.

One primary concern many young adults grapple with is the authenticity of connections made through social media and digital platforms. It's the classic "Instagram vs. Reality" dilemma, but with a twist: "Is this person real or just really good at Photoshop?"

The ultimate goal of engaging social media content is to encourage interaction and conversation. It's not just about broadcasting your thoughts but inviting others to join the conversation. These interactions can lead to a sense of community.

In our current situation, social media platforms have a vast and undeniable influence on nearly every aspect of life, especially young people. Once considered a revolutionary way to connect and communicate, social media has evolved into a complex space where we constantly compare, curate, and judge. For many, it has become a place where likes, comments, and followers measure self-worth and social abilities. This chapter seeks to explore the impact of social media on our ability to connect, offering insights and strategies to help you rediscover and embrace heartfelt, face-to-face interactions.

The Social Media Effect and Our Feelings

Think of a moment when you were scrolling through social media, and you caught yourself feeling... well, feeling something. Maybe it's a twinge of FOMO (Fear of Missing Out) when you see your friends at a concert you weren't invited to. Or perhaps it's that competitive spark when someone posts about their latest achievement. Here is the thing – most people scroll past these feelings without a second thought. But what if we paused and reflected on these moments instead of brushing them off? These fleeting emotions- envy, joy, or motivation—reveal our deeper desires and insecurities. By paying attention to how we feel as we scroll, we can turn those emotions into insights, helping us better understand ourselves and make more intentional choices about how we engage online and offline.

Think of your emotions as notifications popping up on your phone. Just like you would not ignore a text from your best friend, you should not ignore these emotional notifications. They are trying to tell you something important about yourself.

UNDERSTANDING THE "HIGHLIGHT REEL" PHENOMENON AND HOW IT WARPS REALITY

One of the first and most important realizations when it comes to understanding social media's impact on social skills is recognizing how it presents a distorted version of reality. Social media is, by design, a "highlight reel." People share what they want others to see, often focusing on the positive moments while leaving out struggles, challenges, or mundane everyday moments. This selective sharing creates a space where perfection and excitement are amplified, and flaws or normalcy are hidden from view. It is easy to scroll through your feed and assume that everyone else has it all together—that their lives are more attractive, their friendships are stronger, or their social lives are more fulfilling. But just like in movies or television, what you see is only a carefully curated sliver of someone's experience.

Instead of scrolling through social media aimlessly, consider limiting your time on these platforms and seeking opportunities to reflect on your reality, both the ups and the downs. It's important to ground yourself in the idea that a fulfilling life isn't always perfectly curated, and meaningful connections don't rely on how "shareable" they are. Living with this perspective can relieve some of the pressure to portray a certain image, freeing you to approach conversations and interactions more authentically and relaxedly.

Social media often pressures us to "perform" a version of ourselves that we believe others will find impressive or interesting. This pressure can translate into real-life conversations, making us feel that we must act or speak in certain ways to be liked or accepted. But authentic relationships aren't built on performances but on real, honest exchanges that reveal who you truly are. When you stop trying to impress and instead focus on sharing your honest thoughts, interests, and vulnerabilities, you open the door to deeper, more meaningful interactions.

Shifting from performance to real sharing requires a change in mindset. Instead of viewing conversations as a stage where you need to perform, consider them opportunities to connect and understand. You don't have to have a perfect story or a witty comeback ready; sharing something simple about your day, your interests, or even something you're curious about is enough. This kind of authenticity is refreshing in a world where so many interactions are filtered and calculated. It allows you to connect with others based on who you are rather than the version of yourself that you feel pressured to present.

By redefining your social goals and focusing on quality rather than quantity, you're setting a new standard for what it means to be successful in social interactions. Celebrate small victories in your social life. These moments are more valuable than online admiration because they are built on good interactions rather than superficial approval.

MANAGING SOCIAL MEDIA ANXIETY BY SETTING BOUNDARIES

A significant challenge in today's social landscape is the pervasive anxiety that social media can create. The pressure to keep up with others, post content that gets attention, and maintain a particular image can be exhausting. Social media anxiety can seep into in-person interactions, making it difficult to feel comfortable and confident. Setting healthy boundaries with social media is one of the most effective ways to reclaim your mental and emotional well-being, giving you the space to focus on real-life connections.

Establishing boundaries with social media can involve various approaches. Limiting the time you spend on these platforms each day can prevent the urge to compare yourself to others constantly. Many people find it helpful to designate specific times during the day for checking social media, allowing them to be more present and engaged in their offline lives. Taking occasional breaks from social media, whether for a day, a weekend, or even longer—can also help reset your mind and give you a fresh perspective on what truly matters.

Switching up your feed (algorithm) can further alleviate social media anxiety. Unfollow accounts that make you feel insecure or pressured, and instead follow those that inspire positivity and growth. By managing your digital environment, you can reduce the triggers for comparison and create a healthier online experience. Over time, these boundaries will help you feel less burdened by social media, enabling you to approach real-life interactions with greater confidence and peace of mind.

ONLINE VIBES: BODY LANGUAGE DURING VIDEO CALLS

Have you ever wondered how much of "you" comes across on a screen? In a world where friendships, classes, and even job interviews unfold through tiny boxes on Zoom, your presence matters as much as if you were sitting across from someone in person. The challenge? Screens strip away nuances—your posture, a friendly handshake, or subtle facial expressions, that help people feel connected to you. But here is the secret: mastering your body language online can make you stand out, create stronger connections, and leave a lasting impression, even in a virtual room.

While someone might not be able to tell if you're nervously tapping your foot under the table during a Zoom call, they can notice your facial expressions, eye contact, posture, and how you present yourself on-screen. These visual cues still shape the vibe of the conversation and how you come across to others.

Imagine a typical video call. You log in, and the first thing people see isn't necessarily the words you're about to say; it's your face, your posture, and the environment behind you. Before you speak, they've already gotten a sense of who you are and how you feel. If your face is half-lit or your camera is angled in a way that cuts off half your body, the vibe immediately becomes awkward or uncomfortable. But if you take a moment to set up your space, adjust your posture, and ensure your face is well-lit, you instantly create a more engaging presence on-screen, even without saying a word.

One of the biggest challenges in video calls is maintaining eye contact. In real life, it is one of the most substantial ways to show engagement and confidence, but it's easy to forget where to look in a virtual space. Often, people find themselves staring at the screen, watching the other person's face, but from the viewer's perspective, it can seem like you're avoiding eye contact. The trick here is to look directly at the camera lens when speaking. It feels slightly unnatural at first, but it replicates the effect of eye contact. When the other person sees you looking into the camera, it gives them the impression that you're focused on them, which makes the interaction feel more personal and engaging.

Posture is another critical aspect of online body language. Even though you are sitting in a chair and your lower body is usually out of frame, your posture still communicates a lot. Slouching back or leaning too far into the camera can make you seem disinterested or overly casual while sitting upright with your shoulders back projects confidence and attentiveness. You want to strike a balance where you appear relaxed and engaged, tall but not stiff, leaning slightly forward to show interest when the conversation picks up, and keeping your hands visible when appropriate.

Your facial expressions also carry significant weight in video calls. Since people can only see you from your shoulders up, the expressions on your face become even more important in conveying how you feel. Smiling, nodding in agreement, and keeping your face relaxed are all ways to show that you're engaged and open. But be mindful of exaggerating expressions, as they can sometimes be insincere or forced. In virtual environments, an engaging smile or a slight nod can go a long way in building rapport and keeping the vibe upbeat.

When it comes to gestures in video calls, subtlety is key. In face-to-face interactions, we use our hands to emphasize points or show enthusiasm, but on-screen, large gestures can sometimes feel exaggerated or out of place due to the limited frame. It's better to keep your gestures smaller and more controlled, like using your hands to make a point or express an idea when it feels natural but not constantly moving or fidgeting. Too much movement can be distracting or even tiring for the other person to watch.

Finally, one of the unique challenges of virtual communication is managing the awkwardness of delays or technical glitches. You have probably experienced a time when someone froze mid-sentence, or the audio cut out right when you were about to speak. These moments can feel uncomfortable, but your body language can help ease the tension. Stay calm, smile, and acknowledge the glitch with a lighthearted comment. It shows that you are flexible and can encourage a bright and optimistic tone when technology doesn't cooperate.

In many ways, the key to projecting positive body language during video calls is the same as in real life; be aware of how you present your-self and focus on conveying openness, confidence, and attentiveness. The difference is that online, you need to be even more intentional about it because your range of nonverbal communication is limited to what fits on the screen. With a bit of practice, though, you will find that it's entirely possible to create a robust and positive vibe online just as quickly as you would in person. By mastering these small yet impactful techniques, you create a sense of ease and approachability that helps you talk to anyone, no matter what the medium.

Time to Reflect and Exercises

- What apps or social media platforms make you feel energized vs. drained?
- Which digital interactions leave you feeling connected vs. isolated?

- How does your online persona compare to your offline self?

The Social Media Survival Guide

"Post Pause"

- Before sharing anything, wait 5 minutes.
- Ask yourself: "Why am I really posting this?"
- Consider the potential impact on others and yourself.

The Digital Detox Detection

- Notice when social media starts affecting your mood.
- Set boundaries around usage.
- Create tech-free zones in your life.

PART FOUR
BUILD CONFIDENCE

CHAPTER EIGHT

UNSHAKEABLE: BUILDING SOCIAL CONFIDENCE THAT STICKS

Daily efforts will help maintain confidence and tie nicely into managing social anxiety. The value of these daily practices is immeasurable. When you practice certain behaviors regularly, it becomes second nature. Engaging in brief, friendly interactions daily can gradually expose you to social challenges in a manageable way. Over time, these small steps reinforce positive behaviors, helping you feel more at ease talking to people. Additionally, each successful interaction creates a sense of achievement, increasing confidence.

Engaging in brief, welcoming interactions is another effective practice. Greeting your neighbors, chatting with the barista, or talking with a coworker can significantly build your social confidence. These interactions might seem trivial, but they are valuable opportunities to practice and reinforce social skills. Over time, you'll find that initiating conversations becomes more natural and less intimidating. These small victories accumulate, gradually eroding the barriers of social anxiety.

Self-reflection and improvement are integral to building social confidence. Writing down three positive social interactions daily helps solidify your progress and maintain a positive focus. It also encourages you to identify and challenge negative self-talk. When you catch yourself thinking negatively, replace those thoughts with positive affirmations. For example, if you think, "I'm terrible at telling stories," challenge that by recalling a time when you successfully made a new friend. This practice helps to shift your mindset and build a more positive self-image.

Practicing gratitude is another powerful tool for improving confidence. Each day, note down things you appreciate about yourself. These could be your kindness, sense of humor, or listening ability. Gratitude shifts your focus from perceived shortcomings to strengths, enhancing your self-esteem.

You'll gradually build and maintain social confidence by incorporating these daily practices into your routine. These small, consistent efforts will transform your social interactions, making you feel more comfortable and poised in any setting. With time and dedication, you'll find that social anxiety becomes a thing of the past, replaced by the enjoyment of being involved.

UNDERSTANDING THE IMPORTANCE OF SELF-ESTEEM

Let's start by unpacking what self-esteem really means. In a nutshell, self-esteem is the way you see and value yourself. It's that inner voice that whispers (or sometimes shouts) messages about your worth, your capabilities, and your place in the world. When you have healthy self-esteem, you tend to see yourself in a positive and realistic light. You acknowledge your strengths and weaknesses, but you don't let your flaws define you. You treat yourself with kindness, respect, and compassion, just like you would a dear friend.

On the flip side, when you struggle with low self-esteem, that inner voice can turn into a cruel and relentless critic. You might constantly compare yourself to others and feel like you fall short. You might beat yourself up over every little mistake or imperfection, convincing yourself that you're not smart enough, pretty enough, talented enough, or just plain not enough. And let me tell you, sweet girl, that kind of negative self-talk is not only untrue, but it's also incredibly damaging to your mental health and overall well-being.

But here's the good news: self-esteem is not some fixed, immutable trait that you're born with or stuck with forever. It's a skill that you can learn, practice, and strengthen over time, just like any other muscle in your body. And the more you work on building up your self-esteem, the more you'll start to see the incredible ripple effects in every area of your life.

Think about it: when you feel confident and secure in who you are, you might take healthy risks and go after your dreams. You could ensure to set boundaries and stand up for yourself when someone tries to treat you poorly. Surround yourself with people who lift you up and make you feel good about yourself, rather than those who tear you down or drain your energy. And perhaps most importantly, you're more likely to treat yourself with the love, care, and respect you deserve.

EMBRACING SELF-COMPASSION AND PATIENCE ON YOUR JOURNEY

As you work to build your social skills and confidence in a world heavily influenced by social media, remember that growth takes time. Self-compassion is an essential part of this journey. Everyone makes mistakes, has awkward moments, or feels unsure at times. The goal isn't to be perfect but be kind to yourself along the way, recognizing that you're learning and growing with each experience.

Whenever a social interaction goes wrong or leaves you feeling self-conscious, remind yourself that this is a normal part of the process. Honor every step forward, no matter how small it may seem. By practicing self-compassion and patience, you create a supportive inner environment that allows you to continue pushing forward without fear of judgment or failure.

As you progress, remember that authentic relationships don't require filters, perfection, or validation from an online audience. They thrive on honesty, empathy, and presence. By reclaiming your ability to connect authentically with others, you'll enhance your social skills and enrich your life with the great relationships that can only come from showing up as your true self.

To sum up, self-esteem is a big deal. But do not worry if you're starting from scratch or struggling to see your worth. Building self-esteem is a journey, not a destination, and every tiny step you take toward loving and accepting yourself is worth celebrating.

THE IMPORTANCE OF A POSITIVE ATTITUDE

Having a cheerful outlook is great for creating a favorable social presence. Exuding positivity through your body language makes you more approachable and likable. People are naturally drawn to those who radiate warmth and optimism.

When you catch yourself thinking negatively, challenge those thoughts and replace them with more positive, constructive ones. Lastly, surround yourself with positive influences. Spend time with people who uplift and support you and engage in activities that bring you joy and fulfillment.

Staying optimistic in tough situations can be difficult but not impossible. When faced with constructive criticism, handle it gracefully by viewing it as an opportunity for growth rather than a personal attack.

Respond with openness and appreciation for the feedback. Maintaining a hopeful outlook can help you stay calm and focused during stressful events. Remind yourself that challenges are temporary and can be overcome. Encourage others in group settings by offering words of support and motivation. Your positive energy can uplift the entire group. Lastly, find humor in everyday challenges. A good laugh can diffuse tension and make demanding situations more manageable.

By cultivating a cheerful outlook, you enhance your approachability, encourage positive interactions, reduce stress, and inspire those around you. Your body language and the way you handle challenges further reinforce your positive presence, making social interactions more enjoyable and fulfilling.

OWNING YOUR VOICE IN TOUGH MOMENTS

Imagine you are in a heated discussion with your best friend over a misunderstanding that has been brewing for weeks. Voices are raised, and emotions are running high. You can feel your pulse quickening, and your mind races to defend your side. This is a common scenario for many young adults, especially in our fast-paced, urban environments, where stress and miscommunication can quickly escalate conflicts. Learning how to handle these difficult conversations will reduce stress.

Techniques for Conflict Resolution

When conflicts are unresolved, they can lead to prolonged stress, strained relationships, and a toxic environment. On the other hand, effective conflict resolution reduces stress and helps maintain mental health. When you manage conflicts well, you also build and maintain healthy relationships. This is because addressing issues head-on fosters trust and respect. Additionally, resolving conflicts enhances problem-solving abilities, as it encourages you to think critically and creatively to find solutions. Preventing the escalation of disputes is another key benefit of conflict resolution. When you address issues early and effectively, you stop minor disagreements from snowballing into major conflicts.

Finding common ground and shared goals is another essential strategy. Recognizing shared interests or objectives can turn a contentious discussion into a collaborative effort. For instance, if two team members clash over a project direction, identifying their mutual goal of delivering a successful project can help them work together. Compromising and finding mutually beneficial solutions is also key. This involves each party giving up something to reach a resolution that satisfies everyone. For example, agreeing to a fair chore distribution can be a win-win situation if you and your roommate are arguing about household chores.

Managing emotions during conflicts when facilitating constructive dialogue is a great skill. Practicing deep breathing or mindfulness techniques can help you stay calm. Taking slow, deep breaths can reduce stress and prevent reactive behavior when emotions run high. If emotions escalate, taking a break can be beneficial. Stepping away from the situation lets you cool down and return with a clearer mind. Using calm self-talk is another technique. Remind yourself to stay composed and focus on finding a solution rather than winning the argument. Focusing on the issue rather than personal attacks is vital. Stick to discussing the problem at hand and avoid making the conflict about the person.

Incorporating these conflict resolution techniques into your interactions allows you to navigate difficult effectively. These skills help resolve conflicts, strengthen relationships, reduce stress, and enhance problem-solving abilities.

Handling difficult conversations is an essential skill that can transform your relationships. By incorporating conflict resolution techniques, you will be better equipped to navigate disagreements, reduce stress, and build healthier connections.

Maintaining Composure in Heated Discussions

Maintaining composure in heated discussions is no easy feat. Emotions can flare up unexpectedly, triggering automatic reactions that are hard to control. When you feel attacked or misunderstood, your body's stress response kicks in, making it challenging to keep a cool head. Stress and anxiety heighten these reactions, causing you to feel overwhelmed and less able to think clearly. This often leads to an escalation rather than a de-escalation of the conflict. Setting a calm tone is essential, but it requires conscious effort, especially when emotions are running high. The ability to stay composed helps resolve the issue at hand and preserves the relationship involved.

Pausing before responding is another effective technique. When you feel your emotions rising, take a moment to collect your thoughts before speaking. This brief pause lets you consider your words carefully and avoid saying something you might regret. Focusing on nonverbal cues can also help maintain a calm demeanor. Keep eye contact, but avoid glaring. Keep your posture relaxed and your gestures smooth. This helps you stay calm and signals to the other person that you are open to a calm discussion.

Empathy plays a massive part in difficult conversations. As you put yourself in the other person's shoes, you can better understand their perspective and emotions. This understanding makes it easier to stay calm and respond thoughtfully. Validate the other person's feelings by acknowledging their emotions. You might say, "I can see this situation is frustrating for you." This validation helps the other person feel heard and understood, which can defuse some of the tension.

Acknowledging points of agreement is another way to show empathy. Even if you disagree on many aspects, finding common ground can create a sense of collaboration. Using empathetic language, such as "I understand where you're coming from," demonstrates that you are trying to resolve the issue.

When talking with people, navigating a disagreement about a sensitive topic can test your composure. Suppose a friend mentions a political issue that you strongly disagree with. Instead of reacting defensively, focus on understanding their viewpoint. Ask questions to clarify their position and express your views calmly. You might say, "I see your point about this policy, but I have a different perspective based on my experiences." This respectful exchange allows both parties to share their opinions without escalating the conflict.

Developing lasting social confidence is a transformative journey that empowers young people to connect, thrive, and grow. It is not merely about temporary techniques or superficial fixes; instead, it's about cultivating a foundation of self-belief and adaptability that stands the test of time. By embracing consistent practice, facing fears head-on, and learning from every interaction, anyone can build confidence that becomes second nature.

Equally important is the role of self-awareness and mindset. Confidence grows when individuals identify and challenge limiting beliefs, replacing them with affirmations of worth and capability. Reframing setbacks as opportunities to gain experience ensures that self-doubt becomes a motivator for improvement rather than a barrier to progress.

As you embark on your journey, remember that social confidence is a continuous process of learning and evolving. Surrounding yourself with positive influences can create a supportive environment and bolster self-assurance, making each step feel achievable and rewarding. With commitment, perseverance, and self-compassion, you can unlock the ability to navigate any social scenario with poise, paving the way for enriched relationships and a more fulfilling life.

Time to Reflect

Daily Confidence Rituals

- What are three small, manageable social interactions you could practice daily to build your confidence gradually? How would these moments look and feel?

Celebrating Small Victories

- Think of a recent social interaction that made you feel proud. What went well, and how can you recreate that sense of accomplishment in future situations?

Challenging Negative Narratives

- What is one piece of negative self-talk you often catch yourself repeating? How can you counter it with positive affirmations or evidence from your past successes?

Setting and Achieving Social Goals

- Imagine setting a weekly goal to meet someone new or start a meaningful conversation. What steps could you take to make this goal achievable, and how would reaching it affect your confidence?

Building a Gratitude Mindset

- What are three strengths or qualities you appreciate about yourself that make you a great person to connect with?
- How can focusing on these attributes enhance your social interactions?

CHAPTER NINE

MAXIMIZING YOUR
INFLUENCE

TURN PASSIONS INTO PERSONALITY POWER: HOW HOBBIES MAKE YOU SHINE

Having a variety of hobbies broadens your knowledge and experiences, making you more engaging and relatable in conversations. Engaging in diverse activities exposes you to different perspectives, cultures, and skills, enriching your world understanding. This diversity in knowledge allows you to connect with a more extensive range of people, offering unique conversation topics that can break the ice and sustain engaging dialogues. When you talk about your passions, your enthusiasm shines through, and demonstrating curiosity for others can inspire you. Additionally, sharing interests builds bonds, as people gravitate towards those who share their passions.

Consider expanding your horizons by diving into various activities that enhance your conversational skills. Reading widely across different genres broadens your vocabulary and introduces you to various themes, characters, and ideas that make for compelling conversation starters. Imagine discussing the latest sci-fi novel or a thought-provoking historical biography; these topics can quickly spark interest and keep the conversation flowing. Traveling to new places and experiencing different cultures provides many stories and insights. Sharing your adventures, from trying exotic foods to navigating foreign cities, can captivate listeners and invite them to share their travel experiences.

Participating in group activities like sports or clubs is another excellent way to enhance social skills. Whether joining a fantasy football league, Pickleball, a book club, or a cooking class, these activities encourage teamwork, communication, and camaraderie. Discussing your experiences in these group settings can lead to lively exchanges and shared laughter. Learning new languages challenges your brain and opens doors to new cultures and communities. Imagine the excitement of conversing with someone in their native language or discussing the nuances of different dialects and idioms.

The social benefits of shared hobbies are incredible. Joining meet-up groups or communities can provide a sense of belonging and a platform to meet like-minded individuals. Attending events or meetups related to your interests can lead to spontaneous and engaging conversations. Imagine the thrill of attending a comic book convention and meeting fellow enthusiasts who share your passion for superheroes and graphic novels. Participating in online communities centered around your hobbies and social media groups allows you to connect with people worldwide, exchanging tips, experiences, and stories.

Creative arts like painting, writing, or photography offer a wealth of conversation material. Discussing your latest painting project, sharing a poem you've written, or showing your photography portfolio can captivate and inspire others. These highlight your creativity and invite others to share their artistic endeavors, leading to rich and meaningful exchanges. Adventure sports like hiking, kayaking, or traveling to exotic places are also enjoyable conversation starters. Sharing your latest hiking trail discovery, recounting a thrilling experience, or describing the world you explored can enthrall listeners and invite them to share their own adventure stories.

Interests outside of your daily routine can enrich your life and make you a more relatable conversationalist. They broaden your knowledge, provide unique conversation topics, demonstrate curiosity and passion, and build connections with people who share your interests. By diving into diverse hobbies and interests, you enhance your conversational skills and become someone others enjoy talking to. So, explore new activities, join communities, and share your passions with the world.

CONTINUOUS LEARNING AND PERSONAL GROWTH

Lifelong learning is a treasure of benefits. Staying up to date with the hottest events and trends ensures you always have something relevant to discuss. Whether it is the latest developments in AI or a groundbreaking discovery in medicine, being informed allows you to contribute meaningfully to conversations. This habit not only impresses others but also fosters a sense of intellectual curiosity and engagement with the world around you.

Expanding your knowledge of various subjects broadens your conversational repertoire. Imagine discussing the intricacies of quantum physics one moment and the cultural significance of street art the next. This versatility makes you a captivating conversationalist, capable of engaging with diverse groups of people. Your discussions become more thought-provoking and intellectually stimulating, encouraging others to share their thoughts and ideas.

Sustaining intellectual curiosity is the driving force behind lifelong learning. It is the desire to explore, question, and understand the world in all its complexity. This curiosity enriches your mind and makes you a more dynamic conversationalist. People are drawn to those who exhibit an interest in learning and growing.

Adding new knowledge into your daily life does not have to be a huge task. Start by reading diverse books, articles, and blogs on topics that pique your interest. Whether it's a gripping novel, a scientific journal, or a thought-provoking website, reading broadens your horizons and provides ample material for engaging conversations. Listening to educational podcasts or audiobooks is another excellent way to learn on the go. Commuting, exercising, or relaxing at home turn downtime into productive learning opportunities.

Improving your problem-solving and decision-making skills through personal growth also enhances your ability to navigate complex conversations. Whether it's resolving a disagreement or making a group decision, these skills enable you to approach discussions with clarity and confidence. Cultivating a growth mindset and resilience equips you to handle setbacks and challenges gracefully, making you a more adaptable and resilient conversationalist.

Engaging in activities that promote learning and personal growth enriches your conversational content. Attending lectures or seminars on topics of interest exposes you to latest ideas and perspectives, providing fresh material for discussions. Participating in book clubs or discussion groups allows you to share your thoughts and hear others' viewpoints, fostering a sense of community and intellectual exchange.

Finding volunteer opportunities can be an enriching way to build skills, form friendships, and give back to the community. Start by exploring local resources such as community centers, libraries, schools, and religious organizations that often host programs tailored to youth. Passion-based volunteering, such as environmental clean-ups, animal shelter work, or arts and culture projects, allows young adults to align efforts with interests. Additionally, leadership and skill-building opportunities such as youth mentoring through programs like Big Brothers Big Sisters provide rewarding ways to have influence.

Consider your passions and the causes you care about to find the right fit. Networking through friends, family, and social media can uncover opportunities, while schools and employers often provide access to service-learning programs and corporate volunteer events. Before committing, it's essential to ask questions about time expectations and training and start with short-term projects if unsure about long-term availability. Volunteering benefits communities and equips young adults with valuable skills, boosts confidence, and enhances resumes, making it an influential tool for personal and professional growth.

Volunteering in community service benefits others and provides valuable experiences and stories to share. These activities demonstrate your commitment to social responsibility and offer a wealth of conversation starters. I like to volunteer, show up, keep my commitments, and find community events that interest me.

Continuous learning cannot only make you a more fascinating human but also enrich your interactions with others. By staying informed, expanding your knowledge, and developing new skills, you become a more engaging communicator.

Time to Reflect

- Your hobbies and passions are not just pastimes; they are bridges that connect you to others and make your conversations unforgettable.
- When you share what excites you, your energy becomes magnetic, drawing people in and inspiring them to open up.
- Exploring diverse activities and interests not only enhances your skills but also enriches your worldview, making you a more engaging and empathetic communicator.
- Every book you read, place you travel to, or new skill you try adds a layer to your personality, giving you stories and insights to share with others.
- Cultivating curiosity about others' passions builds stronger connections, as mutual interests form the foundation of meaningful relationships.

PART FIVE
AI & US: NO BS GUIDE

CHAPTER TEN

CHAT SMARTER, NOT HARDER: YOUR AI CONVERSATION GUIDE

Have you ever talked with an AI model and wondered, 'Is this thing actually understanding me?' Here's the truth: while it might feel real, AI doesn't think, feel, or connect like we do—and that changes everything.

AI has been a part of the technology landscape for decades, but everything shifted on November 30, 2022, when OpenAI released its generative AI model, ChatGPT, to the public. Within just seven days, it reached over a million users, a testament to its groundbreaking appeal. This technology has revolutionized how we interact —not only with computers but also with one another—reshaping communication, creativity, and problem-solving on an unprecedented scale.

Unlike a best friend or even a stranger you've just met, AI doesn't bring a lifetime of experiences, emotions, or intuition into a conversation. Humans are shaped by their memories, values, and personal journeys, which influence the way they connect and communicate. Conversely, AI operates based on data and algorithms, mimicking human responses without truly understanding or feeling. This distinction is critical to remember—AI can be a powerful tool, but it can never replace the depth and authenticity of human relationships.

When you are talking to an AI, it's pulling from vast data banks, analyzing language patterns, recognizing phrases, and matching them to possible responses. It is intelligent but not sentient. It's a tool, not a partner. And knowing that is fundamental because how you approach a conversation with AI differs from how you talk to someone. With people, it is about connection. With AI, it is about extraction—getting the answers, insights, or support you need from something that isn't alive but can mimic life very well.

Navigating social interactions has become increasingly complex in the age of AI and digital screens. AI can be complicated these days because it often replaces or mediates human communication, sometimes diluting the authenticity of our interactions. For instance, relying on AI for all your email replies can make interactions feel less personal and hinder the development of connection skills.

Thanks to technological advancements, AI-powered resources are now at your fingertips to enhance your communication skills. These tools can suggest conversation starters tailored to your interests, help you read social cues, and even coach you through managing anxiety in social settings. By integrating these insights, you can direct interactions with ease.

Embracing AI apps does not mean you're relying on a crutch; it's about leveraging available resources to become the best version of yourself. So leap—equip yourself with these innovative strategies and transform every conversation into an opportunity to nurture true bonds.

Let's put that into perspective. Think about how you feel when someone listens to you, paying attention to every word, reading between the lines, and maybe even nodding or smiling at the right times. Now compare that to talking to a chatbot or virtual assistant. When you ask AI a question, it's not listening; it's processing, calculating, and finding the most statistically probable answer to give you. And while this might be useful—hey, it can give you great advice, directions, and help with a report—it's not the same as a human interaction.

So, what does this mean for your conversations with people? It's funny because, in a world filled with technology, the human element becomes even more important. While you can use AI to prep for a big talk or practice language skills, the real skill to master is connecting with people in an authentic way that machines can't replicate.

Interestingly, learning to talk to AI can also help you become a better conversationalist with people. AI requires precision—if you're too vague, it might give you something useless. The same goes for people. People respond better when you are clear, specific, and intentional in what you say. Talking to AI can teach you to get to the point, to express yourself clearly, and to think through what you want to know.

ADAPTING TO AI TOOLS

While AI tools can be handy, remember they are helpers, not replacements for natural human touch. Every interaction online is a chance to show your curiosity, kindness, and unique personality. With a little effort and these tools, you're ready to create solid connections in the digital age.

The role of AI in modern communication cannot be overstated. AI tools have revolutionized how we interact, offering unprecedented ways to improve and streamline our communication. Take an AI-powered language-translation tool. These tools break down language barriers, allowing us to converse seamlessly with people from diverse cultures. Whether chatting with a friend in another country or collaborating with an international team, AI makes it easier to understand and be understood.

TURNING DIGITAL CHATS INTO REAL FRIENDSHIPS

1. Become the AI Whisperer—Use Bots to Create Convo Openers

AI isn't just for information; it's an unexpected social hack. You can use AI to brainstorm conversation starters and even practice responses.

Tip: Ask ChatGPT for a few conversation starters or ideas for unique questions you might ask new people. Get creative: "What's the strangest icebreaker question I could ask?" Use these as inspiration for talking points that make you stand out as someone fun and thoughtful.

Why it works: Not only does this make you interesting, but it also lets you practice before diving into a conversation. No more awkward pauses!

2. Emojis & GIFs: The Secret Spice

Digital communication can seem flat without nonverbal cues. But think of emojis as your new facial expressions and GIFs as body language.

Tip: Use an emoji or two as your conversational "signature." It could be something simple, like 🐨 or 🦥, that represents your vibe. You can even use a GIF that reflects your mood. This personal touch is memorable, and people tend to feel a little closer to those with distinctive styles.

Why it works: With each emoji or GIF, you're helping the other person *feel* the conversation, bridging the gap that screens create.

3. Use "Friend Mode" Texting for Entertaining Chats

Most people stick to surface-level chats. What makes someone truly memorable is when they go a little deeper.

Tip: Share a little bit more than usual, like a funny or unusual story from your day. If you meet someone online, go beyond small talk by sharing something authentic. "Today, I accidentally ordered three coffees, and now I'm running on 300% caffeine!"

Why it works: This feels real, making the other person feel comfortable being real, too.

4. Random Acts of Texting

Surprise messages go a long way in digital friendships. Rather than only texting when you have a specific purpose, try sending a spontaneous note now and then.

Tip: Try sending a "Thinking of you!" text or sending them a meme you think they'd enjoy—something like, "This meme made me think of your dog-loving, chai-drinking self. 😂" Small moments like these make a big difference.

Why it works: It reminds people that you're thinking of them, and it's a gesture of thoughtfulness that's hard to ignore.

5. The 3:1 Rule for Online Conversations

Here's a golden rule for digital chats: ask three questions about the other person for every one thing you share about yourself.

Tip: For example, if you're in a chat group for, say, a book club, and someone mentions a favorite book, you might respond, "Oh, I've heard about that! What's the most mind-blowing part so far?" Then, share something related if they ask.

Why it works: People *love* talking about themselves, and when you give them a chance to do so, they remember you as someone who "gets" them.

6. Create IRL Moments in Digital Spaces

One of the best ways to connect online is by taking things offline. Organize a meetup, even if it's virtual at first.

Tip: In a group chat, mention a virtual game night or study session. "Anyone down for a movie watch-along this Friday?" It gives everyone a chance to share the exact moment.

Why it works: Shared experiences, even online, bring people together, and these events can lead to friendships outside of digital spaces.

These little tricks make digital spaces feel human. Additionally, there are grammar and style checkers like Grammarly. These tools go beyond simple spell-checks. They analyze your writing for clarity, tone, and style, ensuring your message is correct and compelling. Suppose you need to send an important email to a potential client. A quick run through Grammarly can polish your text, making you appear professional and articulate.

Exercise Time: AI Tools for Effective Communication

1. **Identify Your Needs:** Determine what areas of your communication you want to improve (e.g., writing, email management, social media engagement, vacation planning).
2. **Choose the Right Tools:** Select AI tools that match your needs. (At the time of this writing, there is OpenAI ChatGPT, Anthropic Claude, Google Gemini, and Microsoft Co-Pilot)
3. **Implement and Integrate:** Use these tools in your daily communication tasks. Make it a goal to use the models at least ten minutes daily.
4. **Monitor and Adjust:** Track the impact of these tools on your communication effectiveness. Adjust your strategies based on the insights gained from AI analytics.

By leveraging AI tools thoughtfully and strategically, you can enhance your communication skills, making your interactions more efficient, personalized, and impactful. Embracing these modern tools doesn't mean losing the human touch but augmenting your natural abilities to connect more effectively in the technical world.

STAYING HUMAN IN A DIGITAL AGE

I cannot stress this enough. Despite AI's growing role, maintaining a human touch is super important. When you communicate with empathy and understanding, you create bonds that artificial intelligence cannot replicate (at this time in history). Authenticity and credibility come from real input, as over-relying on automated responses can make interactions feel cold and impersonal.

Keep your messages real and add your personality. Embracing this balance allows you to leverage the best of both worlds, creating an innovative and personal communication style while using AI tools to assist in your endeavors.

And here's the twist. Being able to talk to anyone doesn't just mean being a good conversationalist with people. It also means knowing how to communicate with AI. This is your edge; understanding and using all versions of artificial intelligence are skills becoming as necessary as knowing how to drive or type. You can shape the future of AI simply by how you use it. Every time you talk to AI—whether it's asking ChatGPT to help with an essay or using Siri to find a song—you're contributing to how it learns. That means you get to decide how it evolves.

The power is in your hands—how you choose to engage with AI today will shape the kind of world we all live in tomorrow.

Time to Reflect

Chat Smarter, Not Harder

1. **Understanding the Difference**
   - How does knowing that AI is a tool rather than a sentient being change how you approach conversations?
   - Think about the last meaningful conversation you had with a person. How was it different from interacting with an AI?

2. **Balancing Connection and Extraction**
   - Do you use AI for tasks that could be handled through human interaction? Why do you make that choice, and how does it affect your ability to connect with others?
   - In what situations do you think it's better to rely on AI, and when should you prioritize human conversation instead?

3. **Leveraging AI for Growth**
   - Imagine using AI to improve your social skills. What features or tools would you find most helpful for becoming a better communicator?
   - How can you integrate AI's strengths (e.g., conversation starters, social coaching) without letting it replace your own intuition and creativity in conversations?

4. **Personal Connection**
   - Think about a time when someone truly listened to you. What made you feel heard, and how can you recreate that dynamic in your conversations with others?
   - How might over-reliance on AI for communication affect the authenticity of your interactions with people?

5. **Practicing Intentionality**
   - When approaching an AI conversation, do you consider your goals beforehand? How might being more intentional change the outcome of your interactions?

6. **The Bigger Picture**
   - What role do you think AI should play in communication in the future? Should it enhance or replace certain types of interactions?
   - If you could design an AI communication assistant, what features would it have to help you become a more empathetic and skilled conversationalist in real life?

CONCLUSION

As we wrap up together, let's take a moment to reflect on what we learned. When we began, you might have felt overwhelmed by social anxiety, the importance of how you appear, and unsure of how to manage conversations or make new friends, both in person and online. But now, equipped with more than 21 actionable skills, you stand ready to tackle social interactions with newfound confidence and ease.

I hope you've discovered just how powerful communication can be in our ever-changing, AI-driven world. Together, we navigated the shift from outdated strategies to modern approaches, uncovering tools to help you thrive socially. Read this book again and again, to ensure the lessons stay with you, empowering you to build meaningful connections and navigate the world with curiosity, courage, and authenticity.

Put simply, the power of great conversation is undeniable. You have the tools to talk to anyone, whether it's a stranger on the bus, a new friend in your study group, or even a conversation with a chatbot. If you can do that, you're tapping into one of the most universal and underrated superpowers: connection.

Our exploration didn't stop there. We looked at the balance between digital and in-person interactions, the power of storytelling, and practical exercises for social confidence. Handling difficult conversations and enhancing nonverbal communication skills were solid topics, preparing you for more complex social dynamics. Finally, personal development and adapting to AI and modern tools improved your comprehensive guide to becoming a confident communicator.

Personal growth is an ongoing path. Celebrate your progress, no matter how small, and strive for improvement. The skills you've learned here can help enhance your overall quality of life. Believe me, this WILL create more happiness in your life, as it has done for me!

As someone who has battled social anxiety myself (most of my life), moving from city to city, and talking to anyone, I understand the challenges you face. Writing this book has been a reflective personal journey for me, and I am grateful for the opportunity to share these insights with you. Effective communication is not just about talking; it's about connecting, understanding, and growing together. As you move towards better communication, you will grow your courage and resilience!

Now, it's time to put these skills into practice! Start with small steps, like introducing yourself to a new neighbor or having a conversation at the gym. Gradually challenge yourself with more complex interactions. Remember, every interaction is an opportunity to practice and refine your skills.

Thank you for walking this path with me. May this be the beginning of your personal success story, where you choose courage, get out of your house, embrace growth, and create the future waiting for you. I am excited to see the confident communicator you will become and all the new friends you make, talking to anyone anytime and with great ease. Keep practicing, stay curious, and remember that every conversation is a step towards becoming the best version of yourself. **I am in your corner!**

Your Voice Matters

If my book sparked a new idea, inspired you, or even kept you in good company for a while, I'd love to hear your thoughts.

Honest reviews help other readers decide if this book is what they need, and your voice can make all the difference!

Leaving a review only takes a moment!

Thank you for supporting this empowerment mission.

Scan the QR code with your smartphone camera below to leave your review:

Or Use the Link: https://www.amazon.com/review/create-review/?asin=1966339003

With heartfelt thanks,
René Clayton

BONUS SECTION

NETWORKING FOR YOUNG ADULTS – BUILDING BRIDGES IN A DIGITAL WORLD

Networking is often misunderstood as a formal, almost forced exchange of LinkedIn profiles at boring conferences. But for young adults in today's tech-savvy world, networking is a dynamic, flexible, and creative process that can unlock career opportunities, personal growth, and valuable collaborations. This bonus section will guide you through the art of networking, helping you make solid connections while leveraging your curiosity and ambition in both the real world and the digital one.

Why Networking Matters

Think of networking as planting seeds in a garden. Some seeds will sprout quickly, becoming opportunities for mentorship, jobs, or collaborations. Others may grow slowly, transforming into unexpected partnerships over time. Networking isn't just about what you can gain; it's about creating a mutually beneficial ecosystem of support, knowledge, and opportunity.

Challenges

1. **Feeling Awkward or Out of Place**
   - Many young adults feel like they don't "belong" in professional networking spaces, worrying they're too inexperienced or unqualified to make meaningful connections.
2. **Not Knowing Where to Start**
   - With so many platforms and events, numerous networking options can be overwhelming.
3. **Struggling to Maintain Connections**
   - It's one thing to meet people, but staying in touch without feeling like a burden can be challenging.
4. **Balancing Professionalism with Authenticity**
   - Young adults often wonder: How much of my real personality should I reveal? Should I be formal, or is it okay to show my sense of humor?

Let's tackle these concerns with practical advice and strategies.

THE BASICS OF EFFECTIVE NETWORKING

1. Build Confidence by Preparing

Before entering any networking situation, whether virtual or in-person, preparation is key.

- **Know Your Goals**
  - Why are you networking? Are you looking for a job, exploring industries, or seeking mentorship? Clarity will help guide your conversations.
- **Create an Elevator Pitch**
  - A quick, engaging summary of who you are and what you're interested in can make a solid first impression. For example:
    - *"Hi, I'm Jake! I'm a recent grad with a passion for sustainable tech solutions. I've been working on a project to reduce carbon footprints in urban areas using AI, and I'd love to hear about your work in this space."*
- **Research the Audience or Event**
  - If you're attending a networking event or meeting someone specific, do some homework. Check LinkedIn profiles, read up on the organization, or skim through recent news about the industry.

2. Make a Positive First Impression

In both digital and in-person settings, the first few moments of interaction set the tone.

- **Dress for the Occasion**
  - In-person, aim for smart-casual unless specified otherwise. Virtually ensure your background is clean and your lighting is good—professional yet approachable.
- **Practice Confident Body Language**
  - In-person, stand tall and offer a firm handshake. Online, sit upright, look into the camera, and smile naturally.
- **Start with a Compliment or Question**
  - Break the ice by showing true interest in the other person. For example:
    - *"I read your recent article on app development trends—what inspired you to explore that topic?"*

NETWORKING IN THE DIGITAL AGE

For tech-savvy young adults, the digital world offers endless networking opportunities. Here's how to navigate these platforms effectively:

LinkedIn: Your Professional Hub

LinkedIn is more than a digital resume—it's a networking powerhouse.

- **Optimize Your Profile**
  - Use a professional photo, write a compelling headline (*e.g., Aspiring Data Analyst | Passionate About Innovation*), and craft a summary highlighting your skills, ambitions, and values.

- **Engage with Content**
  - Post thoughtful comments on industry articles or share your own insights to position yourself as engaged and knowledgeable.
- **Personalize Connection Requests**
  - Add a brief note when connecting:
    - *"Hi Sarah, I saw your presentation on digital marketing trends and found it incredibly insightful. I'd love to connect and learn more about your work."*

Online Communities and Forums

Reddit threads, Slack groups, and Discord servers can be goldmines for connecting with like-minded individuals in your field. Be active and helpful.

PRACTICAL ADVICE FOR PROFESSIONAL NETWORKING EVENTS

Before the Event

- **Prepare Talking Points**
  - Have a few topics or questions ready, such as industry trends, recent news, or mutual interests.
- **Have Your Digital Contact Info Ready (QR Code, NFC sticker, or Link)**
  - Make sure your LinkedIn profile is up to date.

During the Event

- **Approach Groups Strategically**
  - If you feel intimidated, join groups of three or more—it's less pressure than a one-on-one approach.
- **Listen More Than You Speak**
  - Show interest by asking open-ended questions like, *"What do you enjoy most about your current role?"*
- **Take Notes Immediately After**
  - Write down who you met, what you discussed, and any follow-up actions to keep the details fresh.

After the Event

- **Follow Up Promptly**
  - Send a personalized email or LinkedIn message within 24–48 hours. For example:
    - *"Hi Chris, it was great meeting you at the Tech1X conference. I enjoyed our conversation about renewable energy solutions. Let's stay in touch—I'd love to hear more about your upcoming projects."*

MAINTAINING AND GROWING PROFESSIONAL RELATIONSHIPS

Networking doesn't stop at the first interaction. Here's how to nurture connections over time:

1. Stay in Touch Without Being Overbearing

- Share exciting articles or updates that relate to their field.
- Send a quick message on milestones, like congratulating them on a new job.

2. Schedule Check-Ins

- Reach out every few months with a short message:
  - *"Hi Shanti, I hope all is well! I came across this article on AI in healthcare and thought of you. Would love to catch up when you have time."*

3. Offer Value

Networking isn't one-sided. Look for ways to help others, whether it's sharing resources, making introductions, or supporting their projects.

OVERCOMING NETWORKING ANXIETY

Even the most extroverted people can feel nervous about networking. Here's how to manage the jitters:

- **Focus on the Other Person**
  - Shifting the spotlight away from yourself can reduce pressure.
- **Remember: Everyone Started Somewhere**
  - Even the most seasoned professionals were once beginners.
- **Practice Makes Perfect**
  - The more you network, the more natural it will feel.

FINAL THOUGHTS: NETWORKING IS ABOUT RELATIONSHIPS

- Networking is more than exchanging business cards or collecting LinkedIn connections. It's about creating authentic, lasting relationships built on trust, shared interests, and mutual support. By being intentional, prepared, and proactive, you'll find that networking can be an exciting and rewarding journey that will open doors to opportunities you might not have imagined.

- Remember, every conversation is a step forward. So, take a deep breath, smile, and start building your bridge to the future.

DAILY QUESTIONS TO CENTER YOURSELF

1. **What energy am I bringing to conversations today?**
   - Check your emotional weather
   - Consider how your digital interactions affect your mood
   - Reset if needed with a short walk or music break
2. **How can I stay curious about others?**
   - Everyone has a story waiting to be uncovered
   - What can this person teach me?
   - What makes them light up when they talk?
3. **Where can I find common ground?**
   - What shared experiences can we share?
   - How can I bridge generational or cultural gaps?
   - What connects us beyond our differences?
4. **How can I be fully present?**
   - Can I set aside my phone?
   - Am I listening to understand or just to respond?
   - What might I miss if I'm mentally elsewhere?

5. **What value can I add to each interaction?**
   - How can I lift someone's day?
   - What unique perspective can I offer?
   - Where can I share heartfelt appreciation?
6. **How can I keep my social battery charged?**
   - What boundaries do I need to set?
   - When do I need to step back and recharge?
   - How can I communicate these needs positively?

REFERENCES

Atske, S. (2024, April 14). *Social media use in 2021*. Pew Research Center. https://www.pewresearch.org/internet/2021/04/07/social-media-use-in-2021/

Ballard, T., Yeo, G., Vancouver, J. B., & Neal, A. (2017). The dynamics of avoidance goal regulation. *Motivation and Emotion, 41*(1), 1–10. https://doi.org/10.1007/s11031-017-9640-8

Brown, C. G. (2020). Ethical and legal considerations for using mind–body interventions in schools. In *Promoting mind–body health in schools: Interventions for mental health professionals* (pp. 113–128). American Psychological Association. https://doi.org/10.1037/0000157-008

Carson-Chahhoud, K. V., Ameer, F., Sayehmiri, K., Hnin, K., van, A. J. E., Sayehmiri, F., Brinn, M. P., Esterman, A. J., Chang, A. B., & Smith, B. J. (2017). Mass media interventions for preventing smoking in young people. *Cochrane Database of Systematic Reviews, 2017*(6). http://onlinelibrary.wiley.com/doi/10.1002/14651858.CD001006.pub3/abstract

Cherry, K. (2021, September 8). Social anxiety coping skills: Best self-help strategies. *Verywell Mind*. https://www.verywellmind.com/coping-with-social-anxiety-disorder-3024836

Covey, S. R. (1989). *The 7 habits of highly effective people: Powerful lessons in personal change*. Free Press.

Eisenberger, N. I., & Lieberman, M. D. (2016). Emotional responses to interpersonal rejection. *National Center for Biotechnology Information*. https://www.ncbi.nlm.nih.gov/pmc/articles/PMC4734881/

Espinosa, E. (2022, August 16). 13 (really) good elevator pitch examples + templates. *WordStream*. https://www.wordstream.com/blog/ws/2022/08/16/elevator-pitch-examples-templates

Friendzone. (2021, March 15). The power of vulnerability in friendships. *Friendzone Blog*. https://friendzone.sg/blog/vulnerability-in-friendships

Gilbert, P. (2001). Evolution and social anxiety: The role of attraction, social competition, and social hierarchies. *Psychiatric Clinics of North America, 24*(4), 723–751.

Gillett, R. (2015, December 18). How to skip small talk and have deep conversations. *Business Insider*. https://www.businessinsider.com/how-to-skip-small-talk-and-have-deep-conversations-2015-12

GoTo. (2023, February 15). How to set up a professional video conferencing background. *GoTo*. https://www.goto.com/blog/how-to-set-up-a-professional-video-conferencing-background

Granovetter, M. (1973). The strength of weak ties. *American Journal of Sociology, 78*(6), 1360–1380.

Hootsuite. (2021, August 11). Create engaging and effective social media content. *Hootsuite Help Center.* https://help.hootsuite.com/hc/en-us/articles/4403597090459-Create-engaging-and-effective-social-media-content

Ignite Visibility. (2022, April 20). 9 brands using social media storytelling the right way. *Ignite Visibility.* https://ignitevisibility.com/6-examples-brands-using-social-media-storytelling-right-way/

Jefferies, P., & Ungar, M. (2020). Social anxiety in young people: A prevalence study in seven countries. PLOS ONE, 15(9), e0239133. https://doi.org/10.1371/journal.pone.0239133

Keltner, D., & Tracy, J. L. (2022). The influence of facial expressions on social interactions. *National Center for Biotechnology Information.* https://www.ncbi.nlm.nih.gov/pmc/articles/PMC9680844/

La Faber, R. (2021, September 12). The power of first impressions in networking. *LinkedIn.* https://www.linkedin.com/pulse/power-first-impressions-networking-richard-la-faber

Martin, E. (2021, March 10). 12 ways to have more confident body language. *Verywell Mind.* https://www.verywellmind.com/ten-ways-to-have-more-confident-body-language-3024855

Morin, A. (2021, March 15). 7 active listening techniques for better communication. *Verywell Mind.* https://www.verywellmind.com/what-is-active-listening-3024343

Morgan, N. (2014, July 30). How to tell a great story. *Harvard Business Review.* https://hbr.org/2014/07/how-to-tell-a-great-story

Owl Labs. (2021, July 7). Video conferencing etiquette: 10 tips for a successful meeting. *Owl Labs.* https://resources.owllabs.com/blog/video-conferencing-etiquette

Piñon, M. (2022). How to have a magnetic personality (15 ways to do it). *Social Confidence Mastery.* https://socialconfidencemastery.com/how-to-have-a-magnetic-personality/

PLOS. (2024, October 3). Friendships drive happiness for single young adults. *Neuroscience News.* https://neurosciencenews.com/friendships-happiness-psychology-27765/

Raypole, C. (2019, August 29). 10 tips for overcoming your fear of rejection. *Healthline.* https://www.healthline.com/health/fear-of-rejection

Regan, J. (2023, May 5). 7 ways to get better at small talk—and why you should. *TIME.* https://time.com/6280607/small-talk-tips-benefits

Segal, J., Smith, M., Robinson, L., & Shubin, J. (n.d.). Body language and nonverbal communication. *HelpGuide.* https://www.helpguide.org/relationships/communication/nonverbal-communication

Swift Kick. (n.d.). Icebreakers: Why are they important? *Swift Kick.* https://swiftkickhq.com/icebreakers-why-important

Van Edwards, V. (2023). The charismatic personality: 12 traits you can master. *Science of People*. https://www.scienceofpeople.com/charismatic-traits

Virtual Speech. (2020, October 5). Cultural differences in body language to be aware of. *Virtual Speech*. https://virtualspeech.com/blog/cultural-differences-in-body-language

Walden University. (2023). The role body language plays in professional settings. *Walden University*. https://www.waldenu.edu/programs/business/resource/the-role-body-language-plays-in-professional-settings

Walsh, L. C., & Nezlek, J. B. (2024). Satisfaction with friendships and happiness among single young adults. *Journal of Social and Personal Relationships*, 41(10), 2345–2362.

wikiHow. (2021). How to fill awkward silences: 15+ useful techniques. *wikiHow*. https://www.wikihow.com/Fill-Awkward-Silences

Willmoth, H. (2024, October 2). Friendships key to single Gen Z happiness, study says. *Newsweek*. https://www.newsweek.com/friendships-key-single-gen-z-happiness-study-1961889

Made in the USA
Middletown, DE
15 January 2025